Dedication

This book is dedicated to Loretta Lepkowski Rainville of Salem, Massachusetts, a good friend who was not only my secretary while I was the Sheriff of Essex County, but has also been the editor of many of the books and articles that I have written over the years. She lives with her husband Roger on Dearborn Street, in a home built by noted horticulturalist Robert Manning. Manning, who was also the uncle of famous novelist Nathaniel Hawthorne, also had a home built for Hawthorne and his mother, next door to his own on Dearborn Street. He not only developed many new varieties of apples and, more notedly, pears in his orchard, but was also co-author, along with John Ives, of *"The Book Of Fruits,"* which was the bible for American fruit-growers for decades. Coincidentally, Loretta Rainville is an excellent cook — especially of cakes and pies — and often tests her delicacies on me, which I always appreciate. As those who know her will testify, she truly personifies sugar and spice and everything nice.

The home of Robert Manning, now owned by the Rainville family, was once the gateway to his world-renowned "Pomological Gardens," where he developed over 1,000 varieties of pears. The great purple beachtree, shown here, was planted by his wife Rebecca in 1876.

©Copyright, Old Saltbox, 1991 ISBN - 0-9626162-2-2

COVER PHOTO: A lithograph of Pilgrim woman offering food to Chief Massasoit at Plymouth in 1621, courtesy of the Gerlach Barllow Company,Joliet, Illinois. From a painting by J.L. Gerris. Photo by Stephen Harwood.

INTRODUCTION

"The way to a man's heart is through his stomach," so goes the old saying, but once the woman won the man's heart, she often remained in the kitchen for the rest of her life. This was especially true during the early settler's life in America. In this country's first homes, the kitchen also functioned as the parlor, dining room, and sometimes even the bedroom. The huts, cabins, and wigwams built by New England's first settlers usually consisted of one large room. The fireplace acted as the stove, and utensils considered a necessity in fireplace-cooking were often unavailable, as were many ingredients needed to compose a decent meal. The meals themselves were served in wooden bowls and eaten with wooden spoons, and as one shocked English visitor to our shores in 1645 commented, *"they use a single knife at mealtime, which they pass around the table."* One fork was in existence in New England in 1630, but the use of forks in eating didn't become popular until the mid-1800s. Our New England ancestors primarily used their fingers in handling food at the dinner table, and the entire family could often be found dipping into a common bowl. There were normally no chairs to be found in these first American homes, only trenchers or benches, which were reserved solely for adult use; in Puritan society the children were expected to stand during mealtimes. Wednesdays and Saturdays were baking days for New England women, and this tradition lasted even into the 20th century. Sunday dinners were cooked on Saturday, because there was no labor allowed from four o'clock on Saturday until midnight on Sunday. In effect well into the 19th century, this law was not observed to give the women a deserved rest, but was strictly enforced only because of commonly held religious principles of the day.

The woman of the house not only had to cook and serve three meals a day for her family, but was also expected to wash all dishes and clothing. Cleaning, weaving, sewing, spinning, knitting, butter-churning, corn-grinding, and water collecting from a nearby well or stream were all part of a woman's daily work. She was also the appointed caretaker of the family vegetable garden, which was often the sole means of keeping her family from hunger. Thanks to the local Indians, corn was introduced to the local diet, and a windmill was erected at Cambridge, Massachusetts in 1632 for the grinding of corn. Another stood at Dorchester in 1633, built by Israel Stoughton, and was water-powered. In 1640, William Trask built a *"mortar-mill for pounding corn"* on the banks of Salem's North River, followed by Robert Burgess of Saugus, who was *"fined for bad corn grinding"* in 1652. Therefore by the 1650s, most New England women were thankfully relieved of the task of pounding their own corn for bread day after day. Except for corn, most Indian dishes didn't set well with the first settlers. One early housewife, Mary Rowlandson, who was taken captive by hostile Indians in 1675, wrote after her release that, *"The first week of being among them, I hardly ate anything; the second week I found my stomach grew very faint for want of something, and yet it was very hard to get down their filthy trash; but the third week, though I could think how formerly my stomach would turn against this or that, and I could starve and die before I could eat such things, yet, they were pleasant and savory to my taste."* The son of the Indian chief brought her *"a pan-cake made of parched wheat, beaten and fried in bear's grease, but I thought I never tasted pleasanter meat in my life."*

"If you can't stand the heat, get out of the kitchen," Harry Truman once said, but it wasn't so much the heat of the kitchen that bothered the early American housewives. Their homes were obviously quite drafty, but smoke always encircled them as they labored at the hearth each day. This problem was controlled by a self-made engineer-scientist named Benjamin Thompson of Woburn, Massachusetts, who invented a stove-cooker *"to prevent the greatest of all plagues, a smoking chimney."* His *"Rumford Roaster,"* as it was called, was manufactured at Salem and was a delight to those who could afford to buy one. Sarah Emery of Newbury had one installed in the house in the mid 1700s, and described it as *"a huge contrivance of brick and masonry. It had several boilers of different sizes, and other devices to facilitate domestic purposes, with apertures under each for a wood fire."* As popular as this new stove was in New England, its inventor never was. When the Revolution began, Thompson, alias Count Rumford, sailed for England to fight as a Tory colonel in the British Army, leaving his wife and baby behind. After the war, however, he was knighted by the king and became the Governor of Bavaria.

It is interesting to note that about the same time Sarah was getting her new roaster, she tells us that *"there has been an exodus of Newbury people to the wilds of New Hampshire."* As Thompson's Rumford Roaster was revolutionizing cooking in many households, the war was beginning and, as George Washington himself said in 1779, *"A wagon-load of money will scarcely purchase a wagon-load of provisions"* — flour alone went from $2.50 per one-hundred pounds to $95.00. Corn prices inflated 10,000 percent, and beef, by some 35,000 percent. Timothy Pickering of Salem, Washington's Secretary of War, said that, *"I just can't make ends meet on my salary of $14,000 per year."* — sound familiar?

Even with the Rumford Roaster, the old cooking fireplace died hard in New England. In 1864, poet Lucy Larcom of Beverly, Massachusetts, recalls fond childhood memories of time spent in and around the fireplace at Thanksgiving time: *"The fireplace was deep, and there was a 'settle' in the chimney corner, where three of us youngest girls could sit together and toast our toes on the andirons...The coffee-pot was set for breakfast over hot coals, on a three-legged bit of iron called a 'trivet.' Potatoes were roasted in the ashes, and the turkey in a 'tin-kitchen,' the business of turning the spit being usually delegated to some of us small folk, who were only too willing to burn our faces in honor of the annual festival. There were brick ovens in the chimney corner, where the great bakings were done, but there was also an iron article called a 'Dutch oven' in which delicious bread could be baked over the coals...If I could only be allowed to blow the bellows when the fire began to get low, I was a happy girl."*

And so, through the fire and smoke of yesteryear, the American housewife — chief cook and bottle-washer — provided all the meals, be it in feast or famine, that made this nation grow to what it is today. This little book, however, is not only about the housewives of old, but about the food they cooked and served — and about the food providers, developers and produce merchant mariners of New England who made this nation THE land of plenty.

Bob Cahill

A typical New England kitchen of the late 1800s, when the cast-iron stove replaced the fireplace and Rumford-Roaster for cooking.
Lithograph by Louis Prang.

I
The Sacred Cod and Blessed Bean

"This is good old Boston, the home of the Bean and Cod, where the Lowells talk only to the Cabots, and the Cabots talk only to God."

John Collins Bossidy recited this catchy poem in a talk at Holy Cross College in Worcester, Massachusetts in 1910, and it soon became a popular New England saying. Baked beans was a staple of the New England diet for centuries, often accompanied by cod in the form of fishcakes at the dinner table. It was the cod, in fact, that initially provided the wealth for merchants like the Lowells and Cabots, thrusting them into America's self-made high society where, as most commoners surmised, they considered themselves too good to talk to anyone but themselves.

Home-port for the prosperous Cabot family in the 1700s was Beverly, Massachusetts, and Beverly was also hometown for the Boston baked bean. *"In those early days,"* wrote Lucy Larcom, Beverly's noted nineteenth century poet, *"towns used to give each other nicknames like school-boys — ours was called 'Bean-Town'...probably because it adhered a long time to the Puritanic custom of saving Sunday-work by baking beans on Saturday evening, leaving them in the oven overnight. After a while, as families left off heating their ovens, the bean-pots were taken by the village baker on Saturday afternoon, who returned them to each house early on Sunday morning, with the pan of brown bread that went with them. The jingling of the baker's bell made the matter a public one."*

"The bean banquet would be supplemented at our table with a loaf of brown bread, thick cylinder-shaped, hot, full of plums, from a bakery on Essex Street," wrote Edward Murphy from neighboring Salem in his book, *"Yankee Priest." "No friends of ours ever dined more satisfactorily on Saturday night, since all of them had exactly the same fare, only that some — a trifle better off than others — were able to afford an extra such as ketchup...On Saturday nights — just around Sunset, portly Mr. Morgan would drive his huge-buttocked old nag Minnie down the street and Whoa her to a neighing stop at each steady customer's gate. Then he'd heave his bulk from his rickety cart and reach back in to lift up the lid of the wooden box on which he had been sitting. The effect, as I now recall it, was like the release of beauteous Eurydice from the underworld by Orpheus...for there in the box stood three big-bellied earthen pots exhaling what seemed to a hungry boy the very acme of essences, the aroma of Boston-baked beans. The glistening brown gems, each bathed in its own ichor of perfection! The spiraling kitcheny savor, putting a tingle in the pit of the stomach and*

sending salivary juices wild! I'd lick my chops, holding our Mom's yellow mixing bowl to receive as much of the treasure as two thin dimes could induce the great Morgan to ladle up for our evening meal.''

Old Minnie,with her trio of pots, and Morgan, considered the *"best bean man in town,"* had passed away when I entered the world in 1934, but baked beans were still the rage of every family as I grew up in Salem. Franks, better known today as hotdogs, were offered up on Saturday night, just as fishcakes were the usual fare on Fridays. In those days, per order of the Church, Catholics could not eat meat on Fridays. Baked beans in a can, as we purchase them today, can't compare with home-made baked beans in an earthen pot, and I have witnessed, throughout the 20th Century,the decline of beans as a staple of the New England diet. As Father Ed Murphy so adequately described it, just smelling the beans in the pot would drive one wild with anticipation. In the days of the Bean Man, Murphy wrote, *"he couldn't pass through our neighborhood without his pots being emptied to the last luscious scoop.''*

In Robert Shackleton's *"The Book Of Boston,"* he writes that, *"the city religiously celebrates Sunday with fishcakes, brown bread and beans, but that old resounding tramp of church-going feet which is characteristic of some other communities, is not so much in evidence.''* Noted 20th Century historian George Francis Dow writes, *"our ancestors were gross eaters and drinkers... the farmers and common people lived much on salt pork, beans, fish and boiled foods...''* Even during the grand exodus of New Englanders to the wild West, with the first covered wagons leaving Hamilton, Massachusetts in 1787, the main ingredient for survival on the trail was baked beans. Once arrived at their destination, homesteaders planted the beans they hadn't eaten along the way, and baked beans with bacon became the traditional Saturday night meal in the Western territories.

The favorite for baking in the southern New England states was the Navy Pea bean, but in New Hampshire, Maine and Vermont, they preferred the Red Kidney, Jacob's, Marafax and Trout beans. Today, there are some 5,000 varieties of beans to choose from, but most Americans seem to prefer the Navy Pea bean for baking.

Although Beverly's poet laureate, Lucy Larcom, might lead us to believe that her hometown instigated the baked bean as a staple in the New England diet, the bean was here long before Beverly was settled. It was, however, of American origin, being an Indian dish transported to Europe by Christopher Columbus's men in the 1500s and then back to America via the Pilgrims and Puritans in the 1600's. Imagine the surprise of New England's first settlers when they arrived here with beans identical to the ones the local Indians were growing in their gardens. The Indians often baked their beans mixed with meat in homemade ovens dug into the ground, and this prompted the first white settlers to add saltpork to the beans for better flavor. When molasses was imported from the West Indies in the early 1600s, it was added to the beans as a sweetener. The most successful earthen bean-pot maker and distributer in the late 1700s and early 1800s, was Lawrence Pottery of Beverly, Massachusetts. A few years after the Civil War there was a grand reunion of veterans in Boston. The vets of Beverly brought a gift to every old Union soldier - a famous Beverly bean-pot. After the reunion, when all the old soldiers returned home, wives and mothers asked where they had obtained the lovely bean-pots, and the answer was *"Boston"*; thus Beverly lost its claim of being America's *"Bean Town"* to Boston, all due to the generosity of Beverly's Civil War verterans.

Beverly is presently struggling to hold onto another claim, being *"The Birthplace Of The American Navy,"* which the nearby town of Marblehead also cherishes. This first American Navy was established by George Washington shortly after the Battle of Bunker Hill and was made up mostly of Marblehead fishermen, but the first officially commissioned vessel of Washington's Navy, an old Marblehead fishing schooner named *"Hannah,"* was docked and fitted out for war at Beverly, thus prompting this age- old controversy between the two towns. Both,too, could claim to be *"Fishing Capitol of America,"* but nearby Gloucester, at the tip of Cape Ann, dearly holds onto this title. The first fishermen settling into the New World camped at Gloucester in 1624, moved to Salem some three years later, and then moved again in 1629 to Beverly, as founders of that community. At about this same time, a rowdy fisherman named Joseph Dallaber was asked by the Puritans to leave Salem, so he rowed across the bay in an empty hogshead barrel, to Marblehead, to establish a fishing colony there. All these Welsh and English fishermen were pursuing a tasty denizen of the deep, soon known to all new Americans as, *"The Sacred Cod."*

The cod, in fact, was so revered that the Father of the American Revolution, Sam Adams, said of it, *"the codfish was to us what wool was to England or tobacco to Virginia, the staple which became the basis of power and wealth."* In 1615, English Captain Richard Whitbourne relates in his journal that, while fishing off The Grand Banks at Nova Scotia, just north of New England, *"more than 400 sail of fishing ships were annually sent to the Banks by the French and Portuguese, since 1578, making two voyages a year, fishing winter and summer."* The English soon joined the French and Portuguese at the Banks, fishing for what they called, *"Baccalew,"* and the Indians called *"Tamwock,"* just other names for that ugly, tasty codfish, better known as, *"the beef of the sea."*

The Spanish and Portuguese especially loved to eat dried and salted cod. English explorer John Smith, while mapping the New England coast in 1614, mentions in his journal that one of his ships was loaded with dry fish for Spain, which brought the crew a small fortune. *"Eighteen men took with the hook alone,"* he writes, *"sixty thousand cod fish in a month."* Smith considered the cod fish caught off the New England coast much more delicious than those caught off Nova Scotia and Newfoundland. The latter he called *"Poor Johns,"* a name still prevalent for codfish in many Spanish towns. An earlier explorer than Smith, Captain Bartholomew Gosnold, while sailing around a sandy penninsula in the New World in 1602, had his men lower a net to catch some fish for supper. *"We were battered with cod,"* he wrote in his journal. The place where he caught all these fish was from then on called Cape Cod.

When the Pilgrims settled at Plymouth in 1620, a fishing colony had already been established a few years earlier some 40 miles across the bay at Cape Ann, now known as Gloucester. The English fishermen, known as the *"Dorchester Adventurers,"* dried and salted their catch at Gloucester before sailing back to Europe to sell it. These were only summer residents, who returned home in the fall, but in 1623, 14 fishermen remained the winter and spring *"to employ themselves in building houses and planting corn."* The following summer others joined them to fish, dry and salt their catch and to trade with the Indians. At what is now Stage Fort Park in Gloucester, the fishermen constructed homes, saltworks and other structures for curing fish, but, *"these land men, being ill-chosen and ill-commanded, commenced falling into many disorders,"* so Pilgrims warned owners of the Dorchester Company in England. Myles Standish, the military commander at Plymouth, went to Gloucester in an attempt to restore order, as did Roger Conant, *"a religious, sober and prudent gentleman,"* whom the Dorchester Company owners chose to lead the fishermen at Cape Ann. Conant and Standish couldn't see eye-to-eye, and in 1626, the English merchants abandoned the fishing venture at Gloucester, and most of the fishermen returned to England. Conant, persuading a few of the good fishermen and their wives to stay, found a *"fruitful neck of land"* some 16 miles southwest of Cape Ann, which had better soil for planting and a protected harbor. They all moved to this place, which the Indians called *"Naumkeag,"* and two years later was renamed *"Salem."*

Although America's first fishermen gave up Gloucester as their base of operations in 1626, Gloucester remains synonymous with fishing and is the oldest, and still the most important, fishing port in the nation. Marblehead rivalled Gloucester as America's foremost fishing port until September of 1846, when a storm at the Grand Banks sank most of Marblehead's fishing fleet, drowning 65 Marbleheaders and depleting the town's fishing industry forever. The Grand Bank and Georges Bank off New England are still considered the richest fishing grounds in the world. As early as 1623, Emmanuel Altham of Plymouth Plantation, fishing at Georges Bank, writes to his brother in England, *"In one hour we got 100 great cod, and if we had stayed after the fog broke up, we might have loaded our ship in a week. I think we caught 1,000 in all, and one fish we caught, I think weighed 100 pounds. It was a big a cod as ever seen."*

Even directly offshore of these new American seaside villages, fish were abundant. One of Salem's first residents, the Reverend Francis Higginson, writes home to England in 1629, that *"the adundance of fish is almost beyond believing, of mackeril, that it would astonish one to behold, likewise codfish in abundance on the coast. There is fish called bass, and of this fish our fishers take many hundreds together..."* There is no doubt that fish was the staple food for the first settlers, and in Roger Clapp's Memoirs of 1630 New England, he writes of a Colonial housewife who says, *"Methinks our children are as cheerful, fat and lusty, with feeding upon those mussels and other fish, as they were in England with their fill of bread."* Writes Clapp, *"Bread was scarce, and a dish of meal, salt and water, boiled together, was a great luxury. With fish, wild onions and herbs, they were sweetly satisfied till other provisions came in."*

In order to preserve this abundance of fish in export, to trade with foreign lands , New England fishermen needed plenty of salt. Roger Conant's talent as a Salter came in handy here, as many such Salters were called on to extract salt from the sea, through a process of evaporation. By 1639, there were salt-works in the seaside communities of Salem, Beverly, Ipswich, Boston, Salisbury, Charlestown and Barnstable. Eventually, Barnstable and Dennis on Cape Cod became the biggest salt producers to cure codfish. Barnstable produced some 30,000 tons of salt annually, utilizing windmills with huge sails stationed along the sandy shore to pump seawater into shallow salt pans. As early as 1636, salted cod and codfish oil was shipped out of Salem and Boston to the West Indies, Spain, and France on a regular basis, using 40-ton ketches with square-rigged sails and six man crews. In return, these fishermen turned merchant mariners, would bring home needed supplies such as cotton, sugar and molasses. If New England salt manufacturers couldn't keep up with the need for salt to cure fish and meats, it could also be imported from the West Indies.

Sugar and molasses were made into *"a new vile liquor"* called rum. At the turn of the 18th century, Salem Towne boasted of nine rum distilleries. As historian Sam Adams Drake boldly put it, *"Salem survived on two commodities, salt for the fish and rum for the fishermen."* The most successful fish-monger and merchant trader in the mid- to late 1600s at Salem was Philip English, a French Hugonaut. He owned 42 fish and foodstuff warehouses and 21 fishing vessels that were also used for trading up and down the coast and abroad. In 1692, he and his wife were accused of witchcraft, but managed to avoid the hangman by bribing the jailer and escaping to New York. After Salem's Witch Hysteria, English returned to Salem and rebuilt his merchant fishing business to its prior success, but the ordeal had already brought his wife to an early grave. Another successful cod fisherman was Benjamin Pickman of Salem. It was said that, *"he became a millionaire by the codfish,"* exporting it to the West Indies. He was so grateful to and enamored of the fish that made him rich, that he had gilded effigies of them carved into the side of the stairs in his mansion which he built on Essex Street in Salem. Pickman and other successful fishermen kept their fleets in constant motion, fishing the Bank from late spring to early fall.Filled, then,with salted fish, they would sail for the West Indies before the New England harbors froze over, and sell their cargo in the tropical climes during the winter months. It was a lucrative business, and by 1665 there were more than 1,500 vessels fishing and trading out of twenty New England seaside villages. One hundred years later, the fishing business was still going strong, with 226 fishing vessels built in New England that year, and 150 fishing schooners carrying 600 men, sailing out of Gloucester alone.

Probably the most ingenius of these codfish merchants were the farmers of Boscawen, New Hampshire.These men, who lived inland and never went to sea, nor touched a hook, line or net, still made a substantial profit from the codfish. When winter set in at Boscawen and there could be no more farming for that year, they would venture down the frozen river to Newburyport, Massachusetts in their horse- drawn sleds, where they would purchase frozen and salted cod to sell to Canadians. Using the frozen river as a road, they would pile their sleds high in Massachusetts and glide all the way to Canada where they easily sold their fish at top dollar to the Catholic French during Lent, as well as trading them for loads of furs.

Because of the cod, New England not only was able to feed itself in its infancy, but prospered and became the envy of merchants from every country, especially England. Mother England attempted to steal the cod fisheries from America in the late 1700s after the Revolution, by claiming the Grand Banks, but John Adams managed to talk them out of it. The *"Codfish Aristocracy"* of New England, as these wealthy fishermen were called, would sooner go to war to protect their ugly fish and its spawning grounds, and the English were well aware of the toughness of New England fishermen. If not for the turkey and the eagle, the cod would certainly have been chosen as the nation's cherished symbol. Throughout the 18th and 19th century, images of the cod appeared on American coins and stamps, and in 1773 its life-sized wooden likeness became a permanent fixture in Boston's State House. It was carved from a solid block of white pine by sculptore John Welch and has hung above the heads of the Massachusetts House members in their chamber since 1784. Occassionally stolen as a prank, the cod is always returned to its place in the House chamber, an everlasting symbol of the *"brute creature,"* as Sam Adams called it, that first nourished this nation.

"The Sacred Cod," carved from a block of white pine, hangs in the House Chamber of the Massachusetts State House. Photo by George Dow.

A roadside sign marks the spot in Hamilton, Massachusetts, where New England pioneers headed for the Wild West in covered-wagons in 1787 — with their pots of beans. Photo left is "A Memorial To All Maine Fishermen," by sculptor Victor Cahill, looking out to sea at America's furthest point east, Lands End, Maine.

Rare Old New England Recipes

Beverly Baked Beans
(Roberta Graffam, Beverly, Mass. — a recipe passed on for 5 generations)

- 1 lb. dry white pea beans
- 12 small white onions
- 2 McIntosh apples
- 1/2 cup dark brown sugar
- 1 cup molasses

- 1/4 salt pork
- 1 tablespoon dry mustard
- 1/2 teaspoon salt and 1/2 teaspoon pepper
- 2 cups boiling water
- 2 tablespoons baking soda

Rinse beans thoroughly and place in pot of cold water with two tablespoons of baking soda — soak overnight. In the morning, put on the stove and bring to a boil, then drain and rinse immediately. Peel onions and leave whole. Core apples and slice. Put beans in beanpot, alternating with apples and onions. Mix together: boiling water, molasses, dry mustard, brown sugar, salt and pepper. Slice salt pork through rind about 1/2 way and nestle it down into the beans with the rind exposed. Pour boiling water mixture over beans and pork. Add water to just barely cover beans. Cover beanpot and place in pre-heated oven at 300 degrees. Bake slowly for 6 to 8 hours. Check every hour and add water if necessary to be sure the beans don't dry out. When the beans are plump, tender and brown, they are done.

Beverly Brown Bread
(Esther Marshall, Beverly Cove, Mass.)

- 1 cup yellow corn meal
- 1 cup whole wheat graham flour
- 1 cup rye flour
- 3/4 cup molasses

- 1 1/2 cups sour milk
- 1 cup raisins
- 1 teaspoon baking soda
- 1 teaspoon salt

Mix all ingredients and place in greased pan or mold with cover. Steam for 2 1/2 hours.

New England Bean Chowder
(Maggie Lynch, Lynn, Mass.)

- 1 cup white navy beans
- 1/4 lb. cubed salt pork
- 1 large onion

- 1 large potato
- 1/2 -1 cup flour

Soak the beans for 4 hours and then put to simmer. Coarsely chop onion then brown in a pan along with the pork. Add these to simmer with the beans. Slice the potato and add to beans, simmer until tender. Add flour as needed to thicken.

Rare Old New England Recipes

Boston Baked Beans Burgundy
(Mayor Ray Flynn, Boston, Mass.)

- 2 medium sized cans of baked beans
- 1 lb. bacon
- 1 lb. sweet italian sausage
- 6 large green peppers (chopped)
- 6 medium onions (sliced)

- 1 three-ounce can of tomato paste
- 3 tablespoons molasses
- 1 teaspoon dry mustard
- 2 cups burgundy wine

Fry bacon and sausage separately until crisp, dry and cut into bite-size pieces. Add onions and peppers, and saute for 3 minutes. Place all in a beanpot. adding the beans and other ingredients. Cook uncovered at 350 degrees for 1 hour.

Marblehead Fish Chowder
(Lincoln Hawkes, Marblehead, Mass.)

- 3 lbs. fresh haddock or cod (skinned and fillet)
- 8 medium onions, whole and peeled
- 3 pints light cream

- 3 sticks of butter
- 4 small potatoes
- 1/2 salt pork
- 1 teaspoon each, salt and pepper

Boil onions and potatoes separately and save water. Simmer fish and salt pork in frying pan for 15 minutes. Remove and place in saucepan, adding light cream, butter, onions, potatoes, and drippings of fish from frying pan. Mix in water from boiling onions and potatoes. Serve hot or save it for a day, when it will taste even better.

Webster's Fish Chowder
(Daniel Webster, Marshfield, Mass.)

- 5 codfish, filleted but not skinned, and keep the heads
- 3/4 lbs. salt pork, in thin slices
- 6 potatoes, boiled

- 1/2 qt. of boiling milk
- 1 onion, boiled
- 1/2 teaspoon of pepper

Add water and layer the fish. Boil for 25 minutes, then add all other ingredients and boil for 5 more minutes. Add 5 hard crackers, and serve.

II
Too Many Cooks

"Thy name is Hasty Pudding! Thus our Sires were wont to greet thee, fumming from their fires. In haste the boiling caldron o'er the blaze receives and cooks the ready powdered maize. In haste 'tis served, and then in equal haste, with cooling milk we make the sweet repast."

Hasty Pudding is perhaps better known as Indian Pudding. Made from corn (or *"maize"* as the Indians called it,) it was just one of the many food dishes the Indians introduced to the Pilgrims and Puritans when these new-comers first settled New England. Succotash, made from mixing beans and corn, was an Indian favorite, and *"pone"* was a popular Indian porridge made by boiling water with ground corn. Indians of Massachusetts, Rhode Island, and New Hampshire cultivated corn and other vegetables such as peas, beans, squash and pumpkins, long before the white-man came to settle. In fact, when the Pilgrims first landed at Provincetown on Cape Cod in November of 1620, before settling at Plymouth, they stole ears of corn from the Indians. The Indians had buried it for the winter under mounds of earth when Myles Standish and his men stumbled upon it. *"We dug up a basket of corn, four bushells, some in eares, faire and good, of diverce colours. We filled up a kettle and our pockets with corn and kept it for seed..."* Iron-ically, it was a local Indian named Tisquantum that informed the Pilgrims that the stolen seeds they planted at Plymouth five months later, would not grow ears of corn unless they fertilized the fields with dead fish and lobster. The local Indians, in fact, taught the starving Pilgrims how to fish for eels in the freshwater streams and rivers, how to locate edible wild plants in the woods, like Indian turnip and cranberry, and how to produce new foods like maplesugar and popcorn.

One of the problems the Pilgrims and Puritans faced when they began using fish and lobster as fertilizer,was that the dogs and cats that they brought from the British Isles would constantly dig it up and eat it. One of the first rules on the Ipswich village books was, *"It is ordered that all dogs and cats, for the space of three weeks (during planting season), shall have one leg tied up. ...If a dog shall break loose and be found doing any harm, the owner shall pay damages. If a man refuses to tie up his dog or cat, and it be found scraping up fish in a corn-field, the owner therefore shall pay twelve pounds damages, beside whatever damage the animal doeth."* Twelve pounds was a very heavy fine to pay in the early 1600s.

Although the Pilgrims and Puritans brought wheat with them from England for planting here, it was soon obvious that the Indians' maize was much better adapted to the New England wilds, especially along the seacoast. Thomas Morton writes in 1666, *"This year much of the wheat is destroyed with blasting and mildew, as also some other grains by worms. On the coast, wheat would not thrive. The Plymouth crop is a failure..."* Governor Hutchinson writes 100 years later, *"little wheat has been raised in Massachusetts for a long time, except in Connecticut River towns."* Although the English often called their wheat *"corn,"* they called New England corn either *"maize"*, as the Indians did, or *"Indian corn."* Because rye could withstand the New England cold winters, America's first bread was a combination of two parts maize and one part rye. *"Brownbread and the Gospel is good fare,"* was an old Pilgrim saying, and the corn-rye combination for bread in the New World was almost as popular as the Gospel well into the 19th century. Prior to the American Revolution, Timothy Dwight writes, *"Rye bread is used in considerable quantities in many places on the Connecticut River...Rye in this region is itself of a dark hue, and is ground without being bolted, the flour being afterwards separated from the bran...It is then mixed with a large portion of the meal of maize, and when baked, is dark, glutinous, and heavy. When a traveller sees this bread brought upon the table at an inn, he looks at it with curiosity and wonder, asks what kind of food it is and is not a little surprised when he is told that it is bread."* After the Revolution, Samuel Goodrich of Connecticut writes, *"Our bread was of rye, tinged with Indian meal. Wheat bread was reserved for the Sacrament and for company; a proof not of its superiority, but of its scarcity."*

Corn bread has always been a New England favorite and was served by the Pilgrims to the Indians at the first Thanksgiving, as was corn on the cob. The Indians had their own bread made from green corn. It was prepared by roasting the ears then cutting off the kernels and patting them into cakes. Both white men and Indians carried bags of plain parched corn with them for instant meals on long hikes, and *"Quadeqina, brother of Chief Massasoit, brought with him a deerskin bag stuffed with popped popcorn,"* for the Thanksgiving Feast. The Pilgrims also introduced butter to the Indians at this three day banquet in the autumn of 1621, but the butter, shipped from England aboard the Mayflower in 1620, was rancid. The Wampanoags spilled it onto their popcorn just the same and loved it. The Indians used the cornsilk to make a tea, and the cornhusks were used to make baskets and bags. The Pilgrims also learned to use the cornhusks in insulating their homes, and it was often the toiletpaper in their drafty outhouses.

The famous Rhode Island Johnny Cakes, originally called *"Journey Cakes"* were created by the Narraganestt Indians and perfected by Roger Williams and his followers. The recipe called for *"soft and sifted white corn-*

meal, scalded with boiling water, kneaded with new milk to three-quarter inch thickness, covered with sweat cream to keep from blistering when placed in the fire, and baked on a red oak board.'' Like Harvard's famed Hasty Pudding, Johnny Cakes could be eaten cold with milk or fried with butter. Another Indian treat was pounded, parched corn floating in milk. It was called Indian No-cake.

The Pastor of Salem's first church, Reverened Francis Higginson, had much to say about food and drink during his short stay in the New World. He arrived in 1629 and wrote back to England that, *''While the first houses were being erected, they grew turnips, parsnips and carrots, both bigger and sweeter here than in England.''* Another visitor, John Josselyn, wrote in his *''New England Rarities,''* that at Salem, *''Peas of all sortes grow, and the best in the world. Also, asparagus thrives exceedingly.''* Higginson also wrote home that *''lobsters weighing 25 pounds, great, fat and luscious,''* could be found in the shallows, and *''the least boy in the Plantation may catch and eat what he will of them...A sup of New England air is better than a whole draft of old England's ale,''* he added. However, in August of 1630, poor Higginson caught cold and died at Salem, from too much of that superior New England air.

Captain John Smith wrote in 1616, a *''Description of New England,''* in which he said that, *''You shall scarcely find any bay or shallow shore, or cove of sand, where you may not take as many clams or lobsters, or both at your pleasure.''* Smith, Higginson and Josselyn made New England sound extremely palatable, when many of the first settlers were nearly starving to death; and if it weren't for the local Indians assistance in planting and hunting, they probably would have been completely wiped out.

At Roger Conant's *''fruitful neck of the land,''* which he and some eight other fishermen and their families settled into, the Naumkeag Indians, living across the North River from them, were most helpful in showing them native planting methods and hunting techniques. Two years after the Conant fishermen had successfully settled in, however, another group of forty immigrants from England, led by John Endicott, arrived to start new lives at Naumkeag. These *''New Planters,''* as they were called, not only came to plant food gardens and orchards, but *''to plant the Gospel in New England,''* so announced Endicott to Conant. The fishermen were religious, but not the strict Puritans that Endicott and his followers were. Endicott had the right under the King's charter to develop a corporate colony at Naumkeag, which he intended to do, but under strict puritanical rules, many of which Conant and his men disagreed with. The two men met for one entire day to iron out their differences - the main one being the growing of tobacco - which

Conant thought was right and profitable. Endicott thought it was a waste of fertile land to develop *"this filthy weed,"* which he considered ungodly. Conant agreed that he and his men would cross the river beyond Indian territory to Beverly and plant tobacco there. This pleased Endicott, and so they agreed that Naumkeag would be renamed Salem, meaning *"peace"* between Old and New Planters. The Indians weren't even informed of the name change, and the peace was shortlived, as the fishermen and New Planters argued over property rights. Finally Conant and his followers moved permanently to Beverly, which the Salem Puritans called *"Beggerly"* out of spite. Adding insult to injury, Endicott's men sailed to Gloucester and removed the oak fish-house that Conant's men had built there, and floated it back to Salem to be rebuilt as The Governor's House for Endicott and his wife.

Wrote Reverend William Hubbard of nearby Ipswich, *"The frost here useth to visit the inhabitants so early in the Winter, and ordinarily tarries so long before it takes leave in Spring, that the difficulty of subsistance is much increased thereby,"* and so it was with Endicott and his New Planters. The Mass Bay Company of England, who had bought all the rights and interests of the Dorchester Company of Cape Ann and Naumkeag, thought it had provided the settlers with adequate protection for the long harsh winters. Every immigrant was supplied with, *"four pairs of shoes and socks, one pair garters, four shirts, two suits of doublet and hose of leather, lined with oiled skin, a woolen suit lined with leather, a cotten waistcoat, wollen cap, black hat, two red knit caps, two pairs gloves, a cloak lined with cotton, and one extra pair of breeches."*

What the Mass Bay owners had failed to supply was enough food to last the long winter, and although the Old Planters and the Naumkeag Indians supplied some food and wild game, it wasn't enough to feed the forty newcomers, and they were forced to eat acorns to survive. *"Sickness early manifested itself,"* wrote the Governer. *"The servants of the Company, for want of wholesome food and suitable lodgings, were seized with scurvy and other distempers."* Doctor Samuel Fuller of Plymouth Plantation was brought to Salem in an attempt to help. He had seen half of 100 Pilgrim settlers die during their first winter in the New World, some eight years before, and he could do little to save the sickly in Salem. Among the twenty or so who died was Mrs. Endicott, the Governor's wife.

In June of 1629, five more ships filled with immigrants arrived at Salem, containing 300 men, 80 women, 26 children and 140 head of cattle. Almost exactly a year later, a new governor, John Winthrop, arrived as well. Aboard the vessel ARBELLA with the new governor was the famed Issac Johnson and his wife, Lady Arbella Johnson, daughter of the English Earl of Lincoln. She didn't last one month in the new Towne of Salem, dying of fever. Governor Winthrop's own son Henry didn't last more than an hour in the New World. Hopping into a canoe in the North River to visit the Naumkeag Indians on the opposite shore, his canoe capsized and he drowned. The Governor was devastated and decided to leave Salem to settle at another safe harbor some 15 miles away. Governor Winthrop gave as his reason for leaving Salem as, *"the place is not large enough to contain three Governors,"* meaning himself, Conant and Endicott. Winthrop had been elected Governor of the Mass Bay Company in London by the corporation owners. He was a wealthy attorney, and the company wanted *"to encourage persons of wealth and quality to remove themselves and families thither."* John Endicott was angry, as Roger Conant had been two years earlier, but the Mass Bay Company attempted to appease Endicott's anger by giving him a large tract of land at Salem Village (now Danvers) where he could plant an extensive garden, and the company sent him hundreds of fruit trees with which to plant America's first orchard. Endicott had a greenthumb and loved gardening, so his dissatisfaction with Winthrop's arrival at Salem was tempered somewhat. Well aware of Endicott's discontent, Winthrop remained in Salem only a week and sailed 15 miles away for Charlestown on the Mystic River, across from what would eventually be the Massachusetts capitol of Boston.

Winthrop considered his first New World meal in Salem quite tasty, *"good venison pasty and good beer,"* but the first winter at Charlestown exhausted the provisions brought from England, and he and his followers were reduced to eating *"acorns, clams and mussels."* One of Winthrop's company, Bartholomew Green, wrote of the 1630 Charlestown experience that, *"upon first coming ashore, we were for a time glad to lodge in empty casks to shelter ourselves from the weather, for want of housing,"* and he hinted that, because of hunger, he and others ate one of the company's dogs.

Governor Winthrop helped to make eating a little easier in the New World when he brought from his homeland a new eating utensil only recently introduced to the English public — the fork. Even as late as the 1630's, people were only acquainted with various types of spoons and knives. They were accustomed to using their fingers to eat most foods, and Governor Winthrop wanted to change all that. He carried the three-pronged fork with him in his jacket pocket whenever he was invited to eat out and made a point to display its use, but it never became popular during his lifetime, nor for some 200 years thereafter.

Of the Winthrop followers who remained behind in Salem in 1630, Endicott tells us that, *"sickness early manifested itself among the newcomers, for want of wholesome food and suitable lodgings."* Endicott also mentions that the cattle that arrived with the new Governor, *"hogs, mares, bulls and goats, were devyded in equall halfes twixt the companie."*. With the exception of *"a bull, a heifer and three or four jades,"* that arrived at Plymouth from England in 1624, the cattle that was divided amongst the settlers at Salem was the first into the New World. Within four years of Winthrop's arrival, there were twenty villages along the New England seacoast containing more domestic animals than people, *"4,000 goats, 1,500 cows, almost as many pigs, and about1,000 sheep."* By 1643, America's first wool mill was in operation at Rowley, Massachusetts, some 15 miles from Salem. The wool was shipped to France and Spain in exchange for wines and fruits. The pigs not only provided meat but also served as tillers, digging up the earth for the farmers to plant seed. In return for livestock and manufactured goods sent from the Mass Bay Company owners in England, the new settlers shipped to England, *"wooden staves and other lumber, sarsparilla and sumach,"* that grows wild here and was used for tea and medicines, *"venison, Indian moccasins, beaver furs, sturgeon and salted cod,"* A beaver fur trading post was established as far north as Augusta, Maine in 1628. The fur was in great demand in Europe for hats, muffs and coats, and beaver meat helped feed the steady stream of new settlers that began arriving in New England, mostly through what was becoming a thriving port at Salem.

Only a few months after Governor Winthrop came and then left Salem for Charlestown, six more vessels arrived at Salem from England, bringing hundreds of new Puritan settlers. Endicott, because of his efforts to assist the newcomers arriving to these shores, was soon known here and abroad as *"The Father of New England."* Also arriving at Salem in the holds of the six new vessels were the vine planter and seedling trees for Endicott to plant what was to become America's first cultivated orchard at Salem Village. These were the nation's first fruits, eventually providing Endicott with another title, *"First Nurseryman of New England."*

John Endicott, "The Father Of New England," *and* "America's First Nurseryman." *Governor's House, built for Endicott at Salem in 1627. This reproduction is located at Salem's Pioneer Village.*

Rare Old New England Recipes

Pompions — 1672

The following is a recipe John Josselyn discovered in New England for cooking pompion, to be served with meat or fish, which he passed on to the cooks of England. It may be the first recorded and published recipe in America, and if not, the first in New England:

"The housewife's manner is to slice them when ripe, cut them into dice, and so fill a pot with them of two or three gallons, and stew them upon a gentle fire for a whole day; and as they sink, they fill again with fresh pompions, not putting any liquor to them, and when it is stewed enough it will look like baked apples; this they dish putting butter to it and a little vinegar, and some spice as ginger, which makes it taste like apple, and so serve it up to be eaten with fish or flesh."

Indian Corn Biscuits — Available 1630, recorded 1686
(Pound Cake)

- 1 pound of butter
- 1 pound of sugar
- 10 eggs
- 1 pint of milk

Add all to ground maize to make thin cakes, and bake slowly.

Puritan Prune Sauce — Available 1636, recorded 1726

- 1 pound of dried prunes (simmer for one hour in water, cool and remove the pits)

Now, boil prunes with 1/2 cup of their juices, and all to boil:

- 1/2 teaspoon of ground ginger
- 1/2 teaspoon of cinnamon
- 1/4 cup of sugar

Stir ingredients constantly as it boils, for three minutes, adding three teaspoons of the juices of the fowl to be served with it — (usually goose or duck). A thick sauce results.

Indian Pudding or Hasty Pudding
Available 1621, recorded 1676.

- 2 1/4 cups of milk
- 1/2 cup of molasses
- 1 1/2 teaspoons of ginger
- 1/2 teaspoon of salt
- 4 tablespoons of butter
- 1/2 cup of cornmeal, ground
- 2 lightly beaten eggs

Scald 1 1/4 cups of milk and stir into mix, pour into 1 1/2 quart buttered pan — let stand for five minutes and pour remaining cup of milk over the top — bake at 300 degrees for 1 1/2 hours.

Rare Old New England Recipes

Rhode Island Johnny Cakes: Thick & Thin
(John Taft, Newport, Rhode Island)
(John Taft, who provided this recipe, insists that Johnny Cakes can only be made with Narragansett Indian corn, stone-ground on granite)

- 2cups of Narragansett corn meal
- 2 cups of boiling water

- 1 teaspoon of salt
- 1/4 cup of milk

Mix meal, salt and water, let stand for five minutes, stir in milk.
Fry 2 1/2 inch cakes on medium-hot, well oiled skillet until browned, then flip.
These are called "thick" Johnny Cakes. To make "thin" Johnny Cakes, cut the salt in half, use 3/4 cup of cold water, and 1 1/2 cups of milk — makes 20 cakes — fry like the thick cakes.

Pilgrim Plum Pudding
(Charlie Sanderson, Plymouth, Mass.)

- 1 1/2 cups flour
- 1 cup brown sugar
- 1 egg
- 1/2 cup of milk
- 1 small carrot, grated
- 1 teaspoon cinnamon
- 1/2 teaspoon nutmeg
- 1/2 teaspoon allspice
- 1/2 teaspoon salt

- 1/4 teaspoon cloves
- 1 teaspoon baking powder
- 1 cup raisins
- 1 cup chopped suet
- 1 cup seeded and peeled small grapes
- 1/2 pound of candied fruit

Mix together (dust fruit with powder flour before adding) steam for 10 hours.

Blackberry Buckle
(Maureen Ryan, Old Lyme, CT)

- 1 pint of blackberries, sweet or tart
- 1/4 cup of butter
- 1/2 cup of sugar
- 1 egg

- 1 cup of flour
- 1 1/2 teaspoons baking powder
- 1/2 teaspoon salt
- 1/3 cup milk

Grease pan with shortening, put in sugar, add egg and add the rest with the milk splashed — spread on Blackberries and bake 40 minutes at 375 degrees.

A statue of Roger Conant, leader of the fishermen, by sculptor Henry Kitson, faces Salem Common. Steve Harwood stands at the spot where Conant and his fishermen finally settled at Beverly, called "Beggerly," by the Puritans of Salem.

Planted by Endicott in 1630, at what is now Danvers, Massachusetts, this 360 year old pear tree just barely survived the 1938 Hurricane. Scions from this ancient pear tree grow nearby on the banks of the Danvers River.

III
America's First Fruits

Fruit trees have been with us since Adam and Eve, and although there is nothing in the Bible that mentions the apple as the *"forbidden fruit"*, it will forever be so identified. The apple was one of the few foods that the Pilgrims and Puritans were anxious to transport from England and develop in the New World. There were grapes, blueberries, rasberries and strawberries growing wild in New England, but not the plump pears, plums, and apples of English orchards. Small starter trees called *"whips"* were transported from England as early as 1622 to the Pilgrims of Plymouth, but nothing in quantity compared to the seedling trees and vine planters delivered to Endicott at Salem in 1630, which included: *"peaches, plums, cherries, pears, apples, quinces, filberts and berries."* These were planted on 300 acres of farmland in what is now Danvers, Massachusetts, just outside Salem, and became America's first cultivated orchard. Endicott called it his *"Orchard Farm,"* and for generations it fed other gardens, orchards and fruit farms throughout America, eventually pressing West through the efforts of such saintly souls as John Chapman, better known as *"Johnny Appleseed"*. To add to the miracle of Endicott's Orchard Farm , one of his first trees is still standing and bearing fruit in Danvers. A gnarled and crooked old pear tree, badly damaged in the Hurricane of 1938, its scions closed in and protected today by a metal fence, lives on from 1630, in tribute to New England's first Governor and Nurseryman.

Another New England Governor, Thomas Prince of Cape Cod, who was also the first banker of Maine, combined politics and pruning and, like Endicott, planted seemingly ageless pear trees. He started his orchard at Nauset, now Eastham, near the tip of the Cape, in 1644. His trees were producing bushels of pears well into the eighteenth century, but none succeeded in making it through the devastating Hurricane of 1938.

Samuel Adams Drake, New England's foremost 19th century historian, speaks of a seemingly everlasting fruit tree at York, Maine. *"Cider-Hill is a classic locality,"* he writes in his *"Nooks and Corners of the New England Coast"*, *"I was struck with the age of the orchards, and by the side of the road is the withered trunk of an ancient tree, said to have been brought from England in a tub more than two hundred years ago. Nothing remains but the hollow shell, which still puts forth a few green shoots. Next to the rocks, it is the oldest object on the road. At a little distance it has sent up an offshoot, now a tree bearing fruit, and has thus risen again, as it were, from its own ashes. This tree deserves to be remembered along with the Stuyvesant and Endicott Peartrees, and there is, or was, another apple-tree of equal age with this in Bristol.''*

It is also said of these whips shipped from England in the early 1600's, that they *"produced a fruit superior in size and quality to that of the Old World.''* Some historians also relate that America's first apple-trees, *"some 500 in number, were exchanged by Endicott in 1648, for 250 acres of land.''* It was, however, a discovery by Governor Winthrop at Boston that disclaims Endicott's apple orchard as being the first in America. When Winthrop and his party were forced to cross the Mystic River from Charlestown to Boston, in 1630, because of a lack of good water *"to make beer,''* they met a hermit named William Blackstone living with the Shawmut Indians at Boston. Winthrop called him *"an eccentric living beside an apple orchard that he planted in 1625.''* The orchard was located at what is now Beacon Hill, home of the Massachusetts Statehouse. As Winthrop moved in, Blackstone moved out, stating that, *"The Lord Brethren are as bad as the Lord Bishops.''* He journeyed to what is now Rhode Island, built a home, and planted another orchard near Pawtucket. When Roger Williams settled Rhode Island, after being kicked out of Salem because of liberal religious views, Blackstone became his friend. Williams and Blackstone preached Christianity to the Narragansett Indians and provided their disciples with apples at every Christian gathering, to keep them interested in learning the new faith. Blackstone had developed a new exceedingly sweet apple in his Rhode Island orchard, which the Indians loved. It was called *"Blaxton's Yellow Sweeting,''* and was instrumental in converting many an Indian to Christianity. Blackstone spent his life tending his orchard and travelling the countryside on the back of a bull, preaching to Indians and riding from tradingpost to tradingpost with large leather bags filled with apples. He died in 1675, just before the great King Philip Indian uprising and was buried in his orchard. He was probably the inspiration for Johnny Appleseed as well. This well-known Springfield, Massachusetts native spent much of his life travelling West to preach the gospel and plant appleseeds, much like Blackstone.

Daniel Gookin, an Indian missionary in New England, wrote of John Eliot, the noted *"Apostle To The Indians,''* that in 1646, *"he visited the nearest Indian village, Nonantum, on the Newton bank of the Charles River, opposite Watertown. Waban, the local sagamore, bade Eliot welcome. He preached a sermon of an hour and a quarter in the Indian language, which his audience declared that they understood. Then came a distribution of apples and biscuits to the children...an excellent method of holding audiences, which Eliot always followed, but which proved a heavy item in the cost of conversion.''*

Not only did the American Indians love the taste of these plump apples newly grown in New England, but so did everyone else. America soon became synonymous with apples — and apple pie. Cider-mills cropped up in every village and town to make sweet cider, hard cider, syrup, apple-jelly, apple-butter and applesauce. Apples were stored in the cool cellars of every home, and apple slices were dried in the rafters of every attic. Within two centuries there were some 1,500 new varieties of apples developed in America. These mostly New England creations ranged from the sweet to the extremely tart and sour, and names for the many varieties were as diverse as the tastes, the most popular being: the McIntosh, Jonathan, Winesap, Newtown Pippen, Granny, Red Delicious, Golden Delicious, Rome, York, Roxbury Russet, Sheep's Nose, Nodhead, Blushing Bride, Beauties, Bailey Spice, Bunker Hill, Hartford Rose, Mountain Sweet, Pine Stump, Disharoon, Old Garden, Nonesuch, Seek-No-Further, and the strange names went on and on.

Probably the apple with the most interesting history or legend afforded it, is the Mike Apple, also known as the Rood Apple or Blood Apple. It is named for a Norwich, Connecticut farmer named Micah Rood, not because he developed this special variety of apple, but because he committed a murder in the apple orchard at Peck Hollow, Franklin, Connecticut. Micah, so legend has it, was not the brightest farmer in Connecticut and had an obsession for jewerly and expensive trinkets. A silver and gold peddler dropped by the Peck Hollow farm one day in 1728 to show Micah his wares. Micah couldn't afford the items he was selling, but decided that he must have them anyway, so he brought the peddler out into the orchard, stabbed him to death, stole his wares, and buried him in the orchard under an old appletree that hadn't produced fruit in years. That spring the old tree flowered, its blossoms not the typical snowy white, but a deep blood red. Then, to the surprise of all the farmers in the neighborhood, that August it produced a quantity of large juicy yellow apples, almost gold-like. To everyone's disgust, however, once an apple was bitten into, it was discovered that it had a drop of blood in it — a red globule like a bloodclot. The blood was at the center of each and every apple on that tree. Nobody knew what the blood spot stood for, only Micah Rood did, and although he was never convicted of murder, the evidence in the Blood Apple was enough to finally kill him with guilt on December 7, 1728. The Blood Apple continues to display the globule of blood near its core, as a reminder to all that no one can get away with murder in an apple orchard.

Apple orchards were considered special, almost mysterious places in early New England, and the apple itself was often considered sacred and symbolic of immortality. The Reverend Samuel Deane once wrote in *"The New England Farmer,"* a highly acclaimed farming publication of the 18th century, that *" apples should be gathered on the day of the full moon. Why may* we not suppose," he asks the readers, "a greater quantity of spirit is sent up into the fruit, when the attraction of the heavenly bodies is greatest? If so, I gather my apples at the time of their greatest perfection, when they have most in them that tends to their preservation — I suspect that the day of the moon's conjuction with the sun may answer as well..." Another minister held in high esteem, also armored with the apple of the 18th century, was Reverend Henry Ward Beecher, father of the famed Harriet Beecher Stowe. "While it is yet flourescent," he wrote of the apple, "white or creamy yellow, with the merest drip of candied juice along the edges, it is as if the flavor were so good to itelf that its own lips watered." Harriet gives us a further insight into this early New Enlgand apple mystique, as she writes in the early 1800s of her childhood in Litchfield, Connecticut: "There were several occasions in course of the yearly housekeeping requiring every hand in the house, which would have lagged sadly had it not been for father's inspiring talent. One of these was the apple-cutting season, in the autumn, when a barrel of cider apple-sauce had to be made, which was to stand frozen in the milkroom, and cut out from time to time in red glaciers, which when duly thawed, supplied the table. The work was done in the kitchen, an immense brass kettle hanging over the deep fireplace, a bright fire blazing and snapping, and all hands, children and servants, employed on the full baskets of apples and quinces that stood around. I have the image of my father still as he sat working the apple peeler."

Another great American writer, Edward Everett Hale, author of "A Man Without A Country," also left behind a note from childhood, further testifying to the importance of the apple in 19th century New England: "I remember that, in more than one winter, when my grandmother in Westhampton had sent us a keg or two of home apple-sauce, the sloop which brought the treasure was frozen up in th Connecticut River below Hartford, so that it was four or five months before we hungry children enjoyed her present."

America's first and foremost novelist, Nathaniel Hawthorne of Salem, gained his education at Bowdoin College, thanks to appletrees and peartrees. His grandfather and his uncle, Richard and Robert Manning, were noted horticulturalists, and Robert willingly paid for his poor, shy nephew's college education. He even built a home for Hawthorne and his mother in the orchard on Dearborn Street, which consisted of over 2,000 fruit trees. Nathaniel disappointed his uncle Robert, because he never took an interest in fruit, except in eating it. Robert, however, won many medals in America and in France exhibiting 1,000 varieties of pears and 118 kinds of apples he had grown, many of which he created himself. The Massachusetts Horticultural Society honored him several times for his "Promological Science,"and for *"procuring and distributing new varieties of fruit."* Manning called his 36 acre orchard, *"The Pomological Gardens,"* which, though planted 200 years later, was coincidentally located only two miles from Endicott's original *"Orchard Farm,"*. Manning, in fact, with another noted New England fruit farmer, John Ives, wrote *"The Book Of Fruits."* Published in 1838, this work was considered the fruit orchard bible of its day, but was never as popular as his nephew's novels, *"The House Of Seven Gables"* and the *"Scarlet Letter."*

Possibly because of Governor Endicott's initial endeavors, Salem soon became the Fruit Basket of America, with almost every resident's backyard containing fruit trees and grapevines. From the *"crude shelters of thatched loghuts and bark tents,"* that Endicott writes about in 1630, Salem became a garden paradise that Edward Johnson describes in 1648: *"The Lord hath been pleased to turn all the wigwams, huts and hovels the English dwelt in at their first coming,"* wrote Johnson, *"into orderly, fair, and well built houses, well furnished many of them, together with orchards filled with goodly fruit trees, and gardens with variety of flowers..."*

Edward Rogers of Salem was given the title of, *"The Father Of Grape-Culture in America,"* when, in his garden and orchard on Essex Street, he successfully crossed a native American wild grape with two Eurpoean vine grapes brought to America from England. He produced 45 seedlings which eventually fruited. Rogers gave these unique hybrids to other farmers to develop further, and thus grape growing and hybridization blossomed at Salem in 1851. A neighbor of Rogers' was John Fiske Allen, who not only wrote extensively on horticulture and the cultivation of grapes, but grew 300 varieties himself. Neighbor Captain Hoffman, also a noted horticulturist, lived nearby on Chestnut Street, a famous thoroughfare lined with sea captains' homes and considered *"the most beautiful street in America."* In the second story of his carriage-house, he developed a *"grape closet,"* as he termed it. Here he preserved his grapes by insulating them with cotton, hair and charcoal. The closet was described as, *"a closely boarded section with the inner surface padded with curled hair, held in place by laths; the heavy door was one-foot thick, and was padded with curled hair held in place with tufted cotton cloth."* Hoffman's closet, however, soon became a military secret. Federal inspectors came to Salem to have Hoffman show them how he built the grape-closet, and it became the model for cold storage by the U.S. Army and Navy to preserve food during the Civil War. It was also the only successful form of cold storage until the advent of the refrigerator and freezer. It is interesting to note that Clarence Birdseye, who discovered the process for blast freezing foods, hailed from nearby Gloucester, Massachusetts.

By the mid- to late 1700s, Salem was a thriving seaport, and almost everyone living in Salem was in some way employed by or associated with the merchant fleet. Although Salem was the sixth largest town in the nation, and second in New England, only 7,000 people lived in Salem, and almost half of them were children. Salem men were almost always at sea, and the town was better known in foreign lands than any other in America. Vessels were constantly departing and arriving in Salem, and soon it was no longer a Puritan English town. French, Irish, Scots, Germans, Scandanavians, Africans, Arabs, Italians, Indians and Chinese flooded the docks and cobblestoned streets. As historian Samuel Adams Drake concluded, *"Salem, by reason of its frequent intercourse with those far countries, took on a tone and color almost Oriental."* The desire to taste new foods from these foreign lands was also stimulated in the seaport towns. One of the first strange edibles brought into Salem port was what sailors called a *"Parmalo."* It was big and round and had course skin. Sailors on Derby Wharf roared with delight as they watched children at the dock, at first eager to taste it, wince with disgusted horror as they bit into it. Captain Shaddock's ship brought these parmalos into port from the tropics, and so this bitter fruit, which no one thought would ever be accepted by the general public, was renamed, *"the Shaddock."* *"Sprinkle a little sugar on them,"* Captain Shaddock urged, *"they're good for whatever ailes you,"* and so he gave away almost a shipload of his namesakes to friends and neighbors. After eating them, the Salemites wanted more. Shaddock obliged them on his next voyage to the tropics, but urged his friends and neighbors to call the bitter fruit by a new name — *"Grapefruit."*

Lemons and limes also became popular, and seamen on long voyages were urged to eat them to avoid scurvey. British tars, in fact, sucked on limes constantly to avoid illness, and American sailors called the British *"limeys,"* a nickname that has persisted to this day. Oranges, of course, were cherished but were rare. They had been introduced to America and Florida in particular, by Columbus in 1493, and then again by Ponce de Leon in 1513, from Spain. To receive an orange as a gift for Christmas or a birthday in New England during the 1700s and early 1800s, was a great treat and an exceptional gift. Juliana Smith of St. Johnsbury, Vermont writes to her cousin in November of 1775, that, *"Brother Jack rode with all due diligence considering the snow and brought an orange to each of the Grandmothers, but they were frozen in his saddle bags. We soaked the frost out in cold water, but I guess they wern't as good as they should have been."*

"The Fruit of Paradise," as South Americans called it, didn't arrive in New England ports until 1870, and then, only by accident. Captain Lorenzo Baker of Wellfleet, Massachusetts, transporting goldminers from New York

to Venezuela, didn't want to return home without a cargo, so he took on bamboo and clusters of a strange looking fruit, which Lorenzo thought tasted like sweet potatoes. When he landed at Boston, all but two pieces of the fruit had rotted, but those who tasted the good fruit, liked it. So, on his next trip to Venezuela, he took on the fruit unripened as cargo. Its skin was golden yellow and just ripe when he arrived in Bean Town. Bostonians went wild about this new fruit, and wanted more. On his third trip, Baker discovered that this Fruit of Paradise was called by the natives, *"banana."*

John Ives, co-author of *"The Book Of Fruits"* with Robert Manning, was also noted for developing many new varities of pears and for producing the popular Ives Grape, also known as the *"Salem Grape."* He also won a silver medal from the American Insititute in 1845 for developing 14 varieties of apples. From his 500-peachtree orchard located where Salem State College now stands, Ives also created the delicious and still popular *"Blood Peach"*. He won many honors and medals from various horticultural societies for producing this peach, but his involvement in improving the size and taste of the poisonous Wolf Peach, also known as the *"Love Apple,"* brought him even greater recognition and a gold-medal of honor from the President of the United States. The development of the poisonous Wolf Peach, however, stimulated a great controversy in America, which is known to this day as, *"The Great Tomato War."*

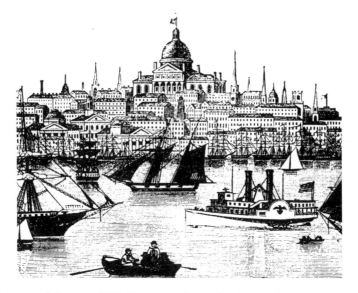

At the top of Beacon Hill, Boston, where the Massachusetts State House now stands, hermit William Blackstone planted America's first apple orchard in 1625. After inviting Governor Winthrop and his party to move into Boston, Blackstone moved out to Rhode Island. An 1857 sketch of Boston from Ballou's Pictorial Magazine.

Rare Old New England Recipes

Mountain Apple Cake
(New Hampshire)

- 6 apples, peeled and sliced thin
- 1 egg
- 1/2 cup sugar
- 1 cup flour
- 1 teaspoon baking soda
- 1/4 cup milk

- 3 teaspoons melted butter
- 1/4 teaspoon lemon juice
- 1/4 teaspoon salt
- 1/2 teaspoon vanilla
- 1/2 cup sugar
- 1/2 teaspoon cinnamon

Beat together egg and sugar, adding the flour and baking soda followed by the milk and melted butter. Next, add in the lemon juice, salt, vanilla, and cinnamon. Spread mix and apples evenly in a buttered cake pan. Bake for 30 minutes in 350 degree oven. Add whipped cream — serves six.

Amherst Pudding
(Massachusetts)

- 3/4 cup butter
- 3/4 pint sugar
- 4 whole eggs

- 5 tablespoons of strained apples
- the juice and grated rind of 1 lemon
- 1 teaspoon nutmeg

Mix all ingredients well and spread evenly in a pudding dish lined with a thinly rolled paste. Bake for 30 minutes in a moderate oven.

Apple Jelly
(Vermont)

- 1 lb. of apples, peeled, cored, and cut in small pieces
- 3 oz. of sugar
- grated rind from 1 lemon (only the yellow peel and not the bitter white rind)
- 1 oz. gelatine.

Add sugar to a pot of boiling water. Sprinkle grate lemon rind over the apples, then squeezing the juice of the lemon over them as well. Boil apples until they are tender, stirring only with a wooden spoon. Add the ounce of gelatine and cook to a pulp.

Applesauce Cider Sherbet
(Rhode Island)

- 1 1/2 cups applesauce
- 1 packet unflavored gelatine
- 1 1/2 cups cider

- 1/2 cup water
- 6 teaspoons raw sugar
- 1 teaspoon lemon juice

Soften the gelatin in hot water until dissolved. Mix well all ingredients, including gelatin, and then freeze.

Rare Old New England Recipes

Apple Custard Pie
(Connecticut)

- 2 apples boiled to a pulp (or 1 cup applesauce)
- 2 egg yolks, lightly beaten
- 1/2 cup sugar (or more if apples are fresh)
- 1 cup milk
- 1 tablespoon flour
- 1/4 tablespoon nutmeg
- 1 pinch of salt

Mix all ingredients and bake in a crust like custard pie at 350 degrees. Egg whites may be used to make a meringue after pie is baked.

Apple Crunch
(Maine)

- 4 tart apples, peeled and sliced
- 1 cup applesauce
- 3 eggs, beaten
- 1/4 cup orange juice
- 1 lemon rind, grated
- 1 cup sugar

- 3/4 cups sifted flour
- 1/2 teaspoon ground cinnamon
- 1/2 cup confectionery sugar
- 3 tablespoons melted butter
- 1/2 cup heavy cream

Mix and bake in one crust for 40 minutes at 300 degrees.

Witch Pears
(Massachusetts)

- 1/2 cup pear juice
- 1 pack gelatin (added to 1 1/2 cups hot water)
- 1 tablespoon chopped ginger

- 4 pears, quartered
- 2 tablespoons lemon juice
- 1 cup white seedless grapes.

Mix and pour all into molds and chill.

Rum Peaches
(Rhode Island)

- 2 lbs. of peach, halved
- 1/4 cup rum (or brandy)
- 1/4 cup butter
- 3/4 cups brown sugar

- 1 teaspoon lemon juice
- 1/4 teaspoon nutmeg
- 1 pint heavy cream, whipped
- 1/3 cup peach juice

Melt the butter in a pan. Stir in peach juice, lemon juice, nutmeg, and sugar. Bring to a boil and then add the peaches and let simmer for 10 minutes. Add rum and simmer for 5 more minutes. Serve warm with whipped cream topping.

IV
The Great Tomato War

America's first millionaire, Elias Hasket Derby of Salem, owned a large wharf directly across from the Custom House as well as many merchant vessels that constantly travelled the world to bring back weird and wonderous items to these shores. In the late 18th and early 19th centuries, there were many other successful marine merchants at Salem and other New England seaports, but none were as daring and as progressive as Derby. It was he, in 1790, who invited the world's most noted horticulturist, George Heusler, an Alsation, to come to Salem as his guest to build the world's most exotic farm. Heusler spent many years here, laying out and planting the farm at what is now Peabody, Massachusetts. He imported many exotic vegetables and fruits from foreign shores, and famous diarist Dr. William Bentley visited the garden in 1801 and described it as a *"kitchen garden,"* with *"oranges, lemons and other rare fruits in the greenhouse."* He also saw *"prickly pears in flower,"* and even , *"ate cherries and brought home leeks."*

Two years before Bentley visited Derby's world famous garden, the Derby vessel MOUNT VERNON docked at Derby's Wharf with a cargo of foodstuffs from the Adriatic. The cargo brought Elias a profit of over $100,000, but something and someone of much greater value to America's future food production was aboard the MOUNT VERNON. Michele Felice Corne, a young and already famous Italian marine artist, stepped onto Derby Wharf. *"I have come,"* he said, *"to paint America,"* and he remained here for the rest of his life. With him, Corne brought the seeds and living plants of his favorite food, which he called, *"Tomatoe,"* but which others called, *"The Love Apple."*

In Salem, the love-apple was also known as *"Wolf Peach,"* and because its juices were considered extremely poisonous, it was also known as the *"Witch Apple."* New Englanders didn't dare touch it nor let their children even near it, and it most certainly was not allowed into their homes. *"If you come too close to it,"* one Salemite observed, *"you can smell the poison."* Therefore, it was a great shock to the adults of Salem, and a delight to the children, when this noted Italian from Naples, sprinkled the little poison balls with salt, and publicly ate them. Be it fate or the plan of Derby, no one knows, but in 1799 Corne lived at the Samuel Pickman House with John Ives, the gardener obsessed with peaches and apples. Corne's plants and seeds of the witch-apple/wolf-peach, obviously stimulated Ives into action. In his Charter Street garden, next to the Olde Burial Grounds, where infamous witch-Judge John Hathorne lay buried, Ives planted and began developing the poisonous plants until, after years of toil, the fruit became plump and juicy. This activity by Corne and Ives at Salem some 100 years earlier would have surely brought them to the gallows condemned as witches by Judge Hathorne. The Judge was, by the way, author Nathaniel Hawthorne's great, great grandfather.

It was about the time Corne came to America that the love-apple was becoming popular as a food in France and Italy. The Spanish had introduced it to Europe in the 1500s when Cortez returned from Central America with seeds from what South and Central American Indians called *"Tomatil."* It was the English who eventually put the *"o"* at the end of it. The red fruit was no bigger than a grape and was considered an aphrodisiac by the Indians, thus the name love-apple. It also looked like a little red heart, so thought Spaniards who began growing it. When the fruit was ripe, they squashed it into a paste and mixed it with olive oil and onions to produce a sauce. This was not the introduction of ketchup to the world, but was the beginning of spaggetti sauce, which eventually, as we all know, became an Italian favorite. Ketchup, from the Chinese *"ketsiap,"* meaning *"pickled fishbrine,"* didn't contain tomatoes until America's Henry Heinz added tomatoes to his long-necked bottles of *"ketchup"* in 1876. Before that, the condiment *"ketchup"* contained fish and vegetable juices, wines, and other solid tidbits like mushrooms and onions. Tomato juice didn't become popular until the Campbell Company condensed tomatoes into a canned soup in 1897.

Marine artist Corne became so adamant in has attempts to popularize the tomato as a food, that he often shunned commissions to paint vessels in order to paint still-lifes of his *"beloved fruit,"* as he called it. Corne also liked to paint fruits that were supplied to him daily from Ives' extensive orchards, and he obviously assisted Ives in his garden behind the house, where the first of the world's juicy baseball-sized tomatoes were developed. It seemed that the more Ives and Corne tried to make people eat it, the more the people shunned it. Local doctors warned that not only was the tomato itself poisonous, but that, *"the fumes from the love-apple, if breathed, are lethal."* In the mid-1800s Doctor James Van Meeter reported that anyone who attempted to eat a tomato would *"foam and froth at the mouth and double over with appendicitis,"* and that, *" the skin of the fruit will stick to the lining of the stomach and cause cancer."* Many ministers warned their parishoners about the ill effects of eating tomatoes, and one Reverend Funk preached that *"love-apples should be feared by virtuous maidens."* Ives, who eventually started his own seed store, gave away tomato seeds to farmers, telling them that the tomato was a fine vegetable and went well at dinner with meats and greens, and even in sandwiches, although the tomato was still considered a fruit then. It wasn't until 1893 that it was officially declared a vegetable by the Supreme Court of the United States, *"subject to vegetable import duties.*"

To speed his promotion of the tomato, Ives ordered a shipload of them from Valpariso, Chile, where they had been consumed by the populace for hundreds of years. The vessel arrived at Salem in 1834, and Ives intensified his planting and distributing of the seeds, preaching that *"the tomato is good to eat,"* and predicting that *"it will surpass all other vegetables as a desired food at the dinner table."*

Even the renowned Thomas Jefferson, after being Ambassador to France, began extolling *"the succulent virtues"* of the tomato, and he started growing them at his Monticello home. He also introduced pasta to America and owned a spaghetti-making machine, but whether or not he topped his pasta with tomato-sauce is lost to history. He supposedly provided seeds of the tomato to George Washington to grow in his gardens at Mount Vernon, but it is said that Martha, once the plants were in full fruit, used the little red balls as decorations for the mantle rather than food for the dinner table. Jefferson once commented, *"I would rather be a common dirt farmer than President of the United States,"* but like farmer Ives, his free distribution of tomatoes and tomato seeds to others didn't seem to advance the tomato as an edible delight.

There were not only preachers and doctors battling Jefferson, Ives and Corne , but other horticulturists and herbalists as well. All realized that the tomato plant itself was poisonous, cousin to henbane and belladonna, known deadly poisons, and that all these plants contained dangerous alkaloids. Some herbalists did conceed, however, that the fruit itself could be rubbed on the skin *"to remove warts, boils and any erruptions upon the exterior flesh."* A popular saying by Doctor James Van Meeter was, *"An apple a day keeps the doctor away, but one love-apple a day will bring the doctor your way."* The most-read magazine of the early 1800s, *"Godey's Lady's Book,"* consented somewhat to the Ives and Corne campaign by telling housewives in an editorial on foods that, *"if love-apples are to be eaten, they must be cooked for three hours, otherwise they may be dangerous to your health,"* and that, *"children should never consume them."* It is interesting to note that, once tomatoes were accepted as a food and were sold in quanity at Quincy Market, Boston in 1845, magazines were extolling *"stewed tomatoes and parsley as an excellent cure for indigestion."*

Disgusted at false claims that depopularized the tomato as a food, a farmer named Robert Johnson announced in the Salem newspaper that, *"At noon on September 26, 1830, I will commit suicide on the steps of the Salem Courthouse, by eating not just one, but a whole basket of Wolf-Peaches..."* This, however, was not at John Ives' hometown of Salem, Massachusetts, but in Salem, New Jersey, where some of Ives' seeds had found their way. Over 2,000 people gathered before the courthouse that day to watch the spectacle. The basket of plump ripe tomatoes sitting beside him, Johnson first gave a speech from the top step. In the crowd was noted anti-tomato antagonist, Doctor James Van Meeter. He interrupted Johnson by shouting, *"The fool will foam and froth at the mouth and double over with appendicitis, and should he survive, by some unlikely chance, he will soon die of cancer."* Johnson laughed and shouted *"Hogwash!"*, then concluded his speech by saying that, *"The day will come when this luscious fruit will form a great garden industry, and will be recognized, eaten, and enjoyed as an edible food."* He reached into his basket, plucked out a big tomato and took a large, audible bite. A young woman in the crowd screamed and another fainted, but Johnson smiled and kept chewing. The town band was at the market, and as Johnson chomped on one tomato after another, they began playing a stimulating march. The crowd began clapping, and by the time he reached for the last tomato in the basket, they were cheering wildly. Doctor Van Meeter left the scene mumbling to himself. The tomato was born! Newspapers and magazines picked up the story of Johnson's triumph, and as one Jersey newspaper reporter put it, *"This was the bite heard 'round the world!"*

Five years later there was a feature article on tomatoes in the *"Maine Farm Magazine,"* in which the editor wrote, *"tomatoes are useful for the diet and should be found on everyone's table."* What John Ives and Michele Corne had attempted some thirty years earlier finally came to fruition, and the plump, juicy tomato, developed by Ives in consort with Corne, became the most versatile food in the American marketplace; eaten raw, cooked, made into sauces, juice, soups and the most favored contiment, its uses seem unlimited. Today it is called *"the orange of the vegetable garden,"* because of its high concentration of Vitamin C. With an offshoot of one of Ives' seeds, a farmer from Calavera County, California grew a 4 1/2 pound tomato in 1893, which was 22 1/2 inches in circumference and 8 inches in diameter, the world's record. For *"the development of the tomato and its introduction in the markets of America,"* John Ives received a gold medal of honor from the President of the United States.

Corne, after painting many vessels in Salem Harbor, moved to Rhode Island, and created more masterpieces on canvas there. Coincidentally, the Peabody Museum of Salem, located across Charter Street where he first lived in the Pickman House, displays the most extensive collection of Corne's work in the world. Corne, however, was more proud of his contribution to the palate than the palette, and his gravestone at Newport reads: *"Michele F. Corne, 1854 — The First Man To Eat A Tomato."*

Rare Old New England Recipes

Tomato Catsup
(New Hampshire)

- 1 qt. tomatoes, mashed to pulp & strained
- 2 oz. sugar
- 1/2 pint vinegar
- 1 teaspoon whole cloves
- 1 teaspoon whole pepper
- 2 teaspoons ground mace
- 1/2 teaspoon salt (or to taste)
- 1 pinch of cayeene pepper

Mix all ingredients and bring to a slow boil until it begins to thicken like cream — about 20 minutes.

Piccalilli
(New Hampshire)

- 1 peck of green tomatoes
- 2 lbs. of onions
- 1 lb. brown sugar
- 1 qt. vinegar
- 6 hot red peppers
- mixed pickling spices, 3/4 box, tied in cloth

Cut up tomatoes and put one cup of salt over, to stand overnight — then grind all.

Tomato Sauce
(Rhode Island)

- 1 qt. tomatoes, mashed to a pulp
- 2 tablespoons flour
- 1 small slice of onion
- 2 tablespoons butter
- 8 cloves
- 1 teaspoon pepper

Stir butter and flour over fire until brown, then stir into the tomatoes. Season with salt and pepper and cook two minutes. Then put through strainer to keep back the seeds. Nice for fish and macaroni.

French Tomato Soup
(Vermont)

- 1 1/2 qts. of tomato
- several beef bones with meat on (remove bones from pot when meat falls off)
- 1 1/2 cups elbow macaroni
- 4 celery stalks, coarsely chopped
- 2 large onions, cut up

Add salt and pepper and cook with added water over low heat for 1 hour or more — serve hot.

John Mansfield Ives, the man who developed the love-apple into the plump tomato we know today, received a gold medal from the President of the United States for adding the tomato to our diet. He also created new varieties of apples, pears, grapes, peaches and squash. Photo of Ives in his favorite buggy, courtesy of his great grandson, John Mansfield.

The 1687 Samuel Pickman House, also known as the Goult-Pickman House, located on Charter Street, behind the Peabody Museum, Salem, Massachusetts. It was here that famous Italian marine artist Michele Corne came to live in 1799, and with Ives, developed the "poisonous" *Wolf Peach into the tomato. Corne claimed to be,* "The first man to eat a tomato." Photo by Steve Harwood.

V
Bringing Home the Bacon

America's first settlers quickly learned to live off the land and sea to survive, and although they were more than willing to try new foods either offered by the Indians or discovered by their own probings, some edibles were immediately discarded or initially avoided because of rampant superstitions of the day. Black shelled sea-mussels, for example, today a New England specialty, were rejected for over three centuries as a food, mainly because the Pilgrims considered them poisonous. When the MAYFLOWER made landfall at the tip of Cape Cod on November 10, 1620, men and boys scoured the beach for food and they had *"a great feast"* of clams, quahogs and mussels, *"very fat."* The clams and quahogs were well received, but the mussels made them sick, *"causing those who ate them to cast and scoure."* The rich meat of the mussels was obviously too potent for their tender stomachs after the long sea journey, and neither they nor their descendants ever ate mussels again. The sand and mud flats of seaside New England are still steaming with mussels, but only within the last ten to twenty years have they been gathered to be served as appetizers in local restaurants. These mussels are, of course, cooked, but when the Pilgrims consumed them as part of their first American meal, they ate them raw — something that even the most courageous shellfish connoisseur wouldn't do today. The Indians, however, did eat mussels, but didn't like them as well as clams and oysters. They considered mussel-meat a cure for piles and hemorrhoids.

"He was a bold man who first ate an oyster," wrote novelist Jonathan Swift in 1731 but at this time in history Cape Cod fishermen were making a fortune on oysters, with over 50 vessels out of Wellfleet alone. They were shipping the tasty bivalves to the Boston market. Our ancestors considered oysters, when eaten raw, to be an aphrodisiac, which obviously enhanced their popularity. Storms eventually depleted the oyster beds of Cape Cod, but they continue to be dredged up for market off the shore of Connecticut. Like with the Indians, clams, either raw or cooked, became the favorite of Pilgrims and Puritans, and were preferred even over lobsters, thus the famous feast of New Englanders is called *"Clam Bake,"* and not lobster bake.

Unlike oysters, which our superstitious ancestors believed could only be eaten in months that had an *"R"* in the name, clams could be eaten at any time, and the mounds of discarded clamshells found along the seacoast by the settlers, proved that the Indians ate clams constantly. The idea of steaming clams was probably a Pilgrim idea to easily force the shells open to get at the meat, especially with the larger, thick-shelled quahogs, also called little-neck clams, that have almost impenetrable covers that open automatically when cooked. Steamed clams and clam chowder are strickly New England specialties, but there is much discussion today, even verbal battles, over which is the *"real"* New England chowder. Those of Connecticut and New York, and even a few Rhode Islanders believe that the soup of the chowder should be made with tomatoes; in Massachusetts and New Hampshire, milk or cream is the preferred liquid. In upper Maine and various nitches of Rhode Island, plain water mixed with the juice of the clams is the only liquid ingredient used to make THE clam chowder. Some also insist that saltpork or pork fat must be added to the chowder, as with fish chowder, to make it authentic. It was a clam digger from Ipswich, home of the most succulent clams, who jokingly experimented one Fourth of July in 1916, at his roadside clam-shack in Essex, with dipping a clam in deep-fried fat — and the fried clam was born. Lawrence Woodman, who sold chewing-gum, potato chips and steamers from his shack to people traveling between Salem and Gloucester in the summertime, was teased by a Gloucester fisherman into dipping a clam in the potato chip grease, and when the fisherman Tarr took a taste of the crisp golden nugget, a new and ever popular food was born. There are more fried clams sold in New England during the summer months today than any other foodstuff. We should give thanks to Tom Tarr for taking that first bite and for having such a great sense of humor — we are forever indebted to him. Non-New Englanders, however, once they see a fried clam, are often squeamish about taking that first bite, but we implore them to dig in and enjoy.

Visitors and locals alike usually have no problem with digging into a lobster, although the shells can sometimes be unwieldy. Lobsters were more plentiful and easily gathered along the shore in shallow water when the Pilgrims and Puritans arrived. Myles Standish, military leader of the Pilgrims, mentions that one morning he had breakfast on *"a pile of lobsters that just lay at waters edge."* Reverend Higginson, first minister of Salem, writes that, *"the least boy in the Plantation may catch and eat what he will of lobsters, many of them weighing 25 pounds apiece."* Lobster, however, was mainly used to fertilize the gardens and, unlike today, it became associated with a poor man's diet rather than a rich man's fare. Passengers of the ship ANNE, arriving at Salem in the early 1600s, complained that, *"the only feast to welcome us was lobster and spring water."* Possibly, as the lobster became more scarce along the waterfront, it became more appetizing. In 1808, Ebenezer Thorndike of Swampscott, Massachusetts, converted an Indian eel-pot into an underwater trap for catching lobsters, so obviously lobsters weren't just laying at waters edge as they were in Myles Standish's day. Thorndike's lobster trap is basically the same devise used today for catching lobsters, and the creature has become even more scarce, in great demand today as the most desired New England food. The increasing demand for lobster by the upper-crust of American society was revealed by Caroline Dall who lived on prestigious Beacon Street in the mid 1800s. *"Boston merchants were very simple then,"* she writes. *"After leaving their places of business, on the way to their homes, they encountered at the head of State Street a wheelbarrow containing boiled lobsters, which were offered for sale... And it was a common sight to see prominent citizens walking down Beacon Street with lobsters wrapped in fresh paper under their arms, and the long scarlet antennae sticking out behind."*

The biggest problem that Colonials had with shellfish was that it had to be eaten fresh and it was never preserved for shipment to villages and towns that were being settled inland at a rapid rate. Alewife, also known as Cape Cod Herring, did travel the streams and rivers inland at various times of the year, and this too, became an early staple of the American diet. Schools of herring were trapped and netted, and then dried, smoked, salted and often pickled to preserve for lean times. Dried and smoked herring was known as *"Skully-Jo."* The fish were individually strung on sticks of cedar, pointed at both ends like big toothpicks, smoked and then strung like candles, twelve to a pack, to be sold at all town and village markets. The sticks were often given to children to suck on all day like candy or to chew a bit at a time when they got hungry. Pickled herring was shipped inland and south to the West Indies and to Europe, and was on the bill-of-fare of many vessels taking long voyages when vinegar was available. The preference seems to have been red-herring; red was actually the color of the fish after it was salted and slowly smoked. The curing, however, never seemed to rid the fish of its poignant smell. As early as 1686, hunters would splash their trail, or the trail of the game they had recently killed, with red herring, to draw wolves off their track. Thus came the expression *"he's dropped a red herring,"* meaning that someone was trying to mislead or interrupt a train ot thought or activity.

Other fish such as cod, flounder, mackerel and haddock were consumed by Colonials of New England constantly and some families ate fresh and dried fish three times a day, every day. The great flounders called halibut were in great demand, then and now, and were considered by many to be the tastiest of all fish. They were much more plentiful in colonial days, the average weight of one fish being some 400 pounds. Gloucester had a thriving halibut industry in the 1800s, each fish caught by hook and line, mostly off Georges Bank. One was caught off Boothbay, Maine in 1807 weighing 637 pounds, after it had been gutted. Such giants are rare today. Blues and striped bass have also been desired eating since the Pilgrims came, but unlike other Atlantic dwellers, they seem to be as plentiful now as ever off the

New England coast.

For those living on the coast in the 1600s and especially for those living inland, the animals of the wilderness were as in-demand for food as were the fish. Deer, elk, moose, rabbit, beaver, muskrat, turkey, and pheasant were hunted constantly by trap or musket or often with bow and arrows like the Indians. Much of the wild animal meat, and most furs, were shipped to Europe in payment for other foodstuffs and merchandise coming here. Salem merchant William Hollingworth tells us that, in 1663, *"fish oil, furs, deer, elk and bear skins are annually sent to England."* New England Indians considered bear meat and its innards the best to be had, but neither Pilgrims nor Puritans acquired a taste for it. The venison of deer was their favorite wild-game meat, and except for the winters of 1667 and 1717, it was readily available to them, *"In ye year 1667,"* Wayland Towne records reveal, *"from ye middle of November until ye middle of March, was the terebilest winter for continuance of frost and snow, and extremely cold, that ever was remembered by any since it was planted with the English, and also through want and scarcity, multitudes of sheep, cattle, deer and other creatures died."* Sidney Perley of Salem writes that, in 1717, because of a great blizzard, *"wild animals became desperate in their cravings of hunger. Browsing for deer was scarce, the succulent shrubs being buried beneath the snow...Bears and wolves in their ravenous state followed the deer in droves into the clearings, at length pouncing on them. Deer were so scarce after this time that officers called 'Deer-Reeves' were chosen in each town, to attend to their preservation."*

Two of the first creatures to become extinct due to excess hunting in less than 100 years of Pilgrims having set foot on American soil, was the wild turkey and the pigeon. Turkey, of course, was served at the first Thanksgiving feast, and since the Pilgrims had never tasted such a delectible bird, it was sought after extensively. Pigeons, so our ancestors thought, although not as meaty as the turkey, were almost as delicious. A Lynn resident in 1637 gives us a glimpse into why the pigeons didn't last long: *"Four to five hours together pigeons flue, and you could see neither beginning nor ending, length nor breadth of millions of birds. They lighted in the woods and broke down limbs, and one man with a pole, killed as many as one hundred dozen in one night. These were pickled and added to the larder."* To find a multitude of pigeons today, one must visit Boston Common. I saw a boy on the Common one day enticing pigeons to him with crusts of bread, then capturing them and hiding them under his long tattered coat, obviously to be taken home for his mother to cook. Therefore, it must be concluded that although the bird has not been hunted for food in New England for over 250 years, there are still people in Boston eating native squab for dinner.

Edward Johnson in his 17th century book, *"Wonder Working Providence,"* gives us a glimpse into how New Englanders were surviving in 1654, and indicated that they were literally out of the woods. *"Flesh is now no rare food,"* he writes home to England from the inland community of Woburn, *"beef, pork and mutton being frequent in many houses, so that this poor wilderness hath not only equalized England in food but goes beyond it in some places for the great plenty of wine and sugar...And in their feasts they have not forgotten the English fashion of stirring up their appetites with variety of cooking their foods."*

Twenty years later, ship master William Harris, writing home to England from Boston, further provides us with indication that the New England standard of living almost equaled that of England, and because of the diligence and ingenuity of our merchants and seafarers, New Englanders were eating better than their European counterparts. *"The merchants seem to be rich men,"* says Harris, *"and their houses as handsomely furnished as most in London. In exchange of fish, pipestoves, wool and tobacco, they have from Spain, Portugal and the Islands, the commodities of those islands; their wool they carry to France and bring thence linen; to England they bring beaver, moose, and deer skins, sugar and logwood, and carry hence clothe and ironwares to Barbadoes, in exchange for horses, beef, pork, butter, cheese, flour, peas, biscuits, sugar, and indigo. Salt they get from Tortugas, and it is clear and white as alum, very sharp and much stronger than ordinary bay salt."*

Less than 100 years later New England was already gaining the worldly reputation of being *"a land of plenty,"* and eating habits, as perceived by the English, bordered on gluttonous. Timothy Dwight seemed a bit disgusted with New England's eating habits and preoccupation with food, when he penned the following: *"The food of the inhabitants at large, even of the poor, is principally flesh and fish, one or the other of which is eaten by the greater part of the inhabitants twice and three times a day. In the country almost universally this is accompanied with smoke-dried beef, cheese, or some species of fish or flesh broiled. So universal is this custom that a breakfast without such an addition is considered as scarcely worth eating...Supper, in most parts of the country, is like breakfast, except that it is made up partially of preserved fruits and different kinds of cake, pies and tarts. The meats used at breakfast and supper are generally intended to be dainties...The proportion of animal food eaten in this country, is, I think, excessive. At entertainments, the dining-table is loaded with a much greater variety of dishes than good sense will justify."*

Of the *"excessive"* meats Timothy Dwight complained, beef and pork were, and apparently still are, the favorites. Although hamburgers, as we know them today, weren't dreamed up until 1888, and then only as a cure for gout and rheumatism, steaks, roasts and beef stews were an integral part of the Colonial diet. It was an English doctor, James Salisbury who prescribed ground beef to his suffering gout patients, *"well done, eaten three times a day,"* and from him we acquired the original name for hamburgers — *"Salisbury Steak."* The old saying of *"eating Humble Pie,"* still prevalent today, comes from the eating of a beef pie during Colonial days which contained the entrails — heart, liver and kidneys — of the cow, and in earlier times, of the deer. It was then called *"Numble Pie,"* numble being another name for the intestines of the animal. There was also a popular beef-stew called *"Lobscouse,"* from the French, meaning *"groin,"* which contained cured beef and pork fat. It was a favorite of New England fishermen and sailors, described once by a passenger aboard ship name Schaw, who said it was *"made up of salt beef that was strung over the side of the ship until fresh and cut into small pieces and stewed with potatoes, onions, peppers and slush, into a stew."* The word *"slush"* is a mariners expression for grease left over in the galley after cooking meat, and from it we get the term *"slush-fund,"* meaning money set aside to buy luxuries. Fresh beef, unless stripped thin and made into hard-tack, would not remain fresh for export or during any extended voyage, therefore, beef soaked in casks of brine with added saltpeter, were usually stashed aboard all vessels — the beef being *"as red as a flannel shirt,"* when it was taken out of a 300-pound cask to soak in water for a day before cooking. Sailors gave the name *"Salt-Horse"* to this red beef, indicating that the meat wasn't always from a bull or cow.

Even the first great cargo ship into New England, the ARBELLA, which also carried the Mass Bay Governor of the New World, John Winthrop, gives us an idea of what these people liked to eat and drink — *"20,000 biscuits, eleven firkins of butter, 40 bushels of dried pease, two hogs-heads of syder, 600lbs. of salt cod, 42 tons of beer and 16 hogs-heads of beef and pork."*

The ARBELLA also carried a hogshead of vinegar, a necessary ingredient for preserving fish, meats, and especially pork which was considered the most precious of foods by the first settlers. Eating pig, *"the forbidden food,"* was taboo to many of the purest of the Puritans coming to the colonies. The love of pork and ham, however, prevailed over the preachings of those who deemed the pig an *"unclean animal not fit for human consumption,"* and the pork smokehouses evolved into nearly sacred places, where mouths would water for a flitch of bacon or a cured shoulder. Pigs awaiting slaughter wandered the streets, and Boston's very first ordinance was for a resident to *"pen his swine"* because they were trampling other people's gardens. As villages expanded into towns, wandering pigs kept garbage-infested streets clean, and it became customary to throw household *"slops"*, leftovers from meals, directly into the streets for the pigs to eat.

Pickled pig-parts and saltpork became lucrative exports from New England and, along with corn, became Newport, Rhode Island's first cargo of trade with Boston. Saltpork became so popular that some were known to wear necklaces of it as a supposed cure or preventative of various diseases. One of America's first historians, John Josselyn, wrote that, *"saltpork will cure a cold stomak,"* whatever that may be. It was also used as an external balm, being pressed on the skin to heal rashes and wounds. Pig grease was often used to make soap. Mixed with ashes and lye, it was a foul-smelling, sticky mess until hardened, but still managed to be a popular New England export to foreign shores.

Bacon was already favored in England; in fact, the saying *"bringing home the bacon"* originated there from a tradition of giving some of it to happily married couples at their one-year anniverary. However, it didn't become popular in America until the 19th century. *"Pork, except the hams, shoulders, and cheeks, is never converted into bacon here,"* writes Timothy Dwight in 1787, *"the sides of the hog are here always pickled, and by the New England people are esteemed much superior to bacon. The pork of New England is fatted upon maize..."*

A traditional meal in New England, even to this day, is pork with corn and applesauce, as well as the old favorite of pork or ham with beans. Along with boiled cabbage, pork or ham was usually served once a week in most New England homes, even through my boyhood — though, as of late, it seems to be out of favor. Many outsiders today still imagine the typical New England meal to be one with pork or corned-beef boiled along with cabbage and potatoes, perhaps enhanced by a few onions or turnips. Often hailed as *"a New England Boiled Dinner"* in restaurants, it has been common fare here for over two centuries. Sarah Knight, travelling by stagecoach from Boston through Connecticut in 1704, provides us with a candid view of such a typical boiled dinner served in restaurants at the time:

"About two in the afternoon, we arrive at the Post's second stage, where the Western Post met us and exchanged letters. Here, having called for something to eat, ye woman brought a twisted thing like a cable, but something whiter, and laying it on the board, tugged for life to bring it into capacity to spread; which having with great pains accomplished, she served in a dish of pork and cabbage, I suppose the remains of Dinner. The sauce was of a deep purple, which I thought was boiled in her dye kettle; the bread was Indian, and everything on the table service agreable to these. I being hungry, got alittle down, but my stomach was soon clot'd, and what cabbage

I swallowed served me for a cudd the whole day after.''

Mutton and lamb were much more popular in colonial days than they are today, and many sheep farms could be found throughout New England. Millionaire Elias Derby sailed in the 700-ton ship **MOUNT HOPE** to South America in 1809 and returned with merino sheep. His intent was to increase American desire for lamb over pork and beef, but over half of his 700-sheep cargo died in passage before reaching his home port. Although Derby eventually started a sheep farm in Peabody, Massachusetts, mutton never caught on as a substitute for pork in New England, only being consumed here on rare occasions.

Salem shipmasters and merchants also attempted to introduce a new fowl to the ever-expanding American diet in 1787, one they hoped would compete with the chicken and turkey. Captain Sanders of the brig **THREE SISTERS** was directed to sail for Africa and procure a male and female bird *"for breeding,''* which he did, but the male bird died in transit. When the female bird arrived at Derby Wharf, nearly everyone in town flocked to the docks to see it. The local newpaper described it as *" a young bird with an exceedingly long neck, about the size of a turkey.''* It was an ostrich. The meat of the ostrich is delicious, so I'm told, and tastes like beef, without the added fat and cholesterol. Because the young female bird lost her mate, no one got the chance to sample ostrich meat in the 18th century, but like the phoenix, the ostrich has risen from the ashes — in 1990, a shipment of African ostriches arrived in the United States and are now being domesticated in order to be bred and slaughtered for meat — we may yet get our chance to eat the big bird.

Whale meat, which has a taste similar to beef, was also consumed by seaside dwellers of the Northeast. From 1820 to 1860, almost every port was home for some 700 whaling vessels, especially Nantucket and New Bedford. I have eaten whale meat many times, before the 1970's government ban on its import into this country, and I'd compare its texture and taste to Yankee Pot Roast. Until the 1970s, it had always been an ingredient of dogfood in the States, and the Japanese still consider it a delicacy, consuming over 100,000 tons of it a year. Although the United States and some 15 other countries have outlawed whaling and the import of whale products, the mass-slaughter of whales still continues and they may, like the American buffalo, some day be virtually extinct.

Meat, be it from animal, bird, fish or shellfish, has always been and will always be, relished by Americans. It was so precious to our New England ancestors, that the meat market was almost always located in the town meetinghouse or townhall, where the important business and politics of the day took place. In Salem, well into the 20th century, I recall visiting Old Townhall as a boy and being fascinated with the great hunks of beef that hung from the rafters on the first floor while the city council debated a controversial issue of the day in the ancient hall above. William Thackar, a visitor to Boston from Philadelphia in 1820, was also amazed that in Massachusetts, the two great loves of the people, meat and politics, shared the same abode — he writes:

"Faneuil Hall, or 'Fannel Hall,' as it is more commonly called or pronounced here, is in Market Square, on the spot formerly appropriated for the sale of provisions — and is used principally for salting and storing their meat; whilst the ground floor is appropriated according to the original intention, and used as a meat market. The hall above, where public meetings are held and where most of the town business is transacted, is nearly the whole size of the building."

It was in this building where people like John Hancock, Sam and John Adams and Paul Revere, not only transacted business, but sowed the seeds of the American Revolution. On the heels of these great patriots, came a Cape Cod butcher, driving his livestock to market each week, bartering over the price of cattle and pork on the main floor of 'Fannel Hall', as Daniel Webster gave a rousing oration in the hall above. He did for meat what Adams, Webster and the others did for American politics. His name was Gustavus Swift and he founded the greatest meat-packing and distributing company in the world. His company, now headquartered in Chicago, still bears his name. In the food world, this meat peddler from Cape Cod, was a true revolutionary.

Shucking corn in York, Maine An 1880 photo by Emma Coleman.

Rare Old New England Recipes

Skully-Jo Fish Bake
(Gloucester, Mass. — 1830)

- Cut cleaned herring or mackerel fish into thick pieces.
- Place in stone jar with 30 pepper-corns and a 1/2 teaspoon of salt.
- Add one blade of mace and a bayleaf.
- Peel one shallot and add to fish.
- Pour in one gill of vinegar, and tie a brown paper tightly over the top of jar with a piece of string.
- Put jar, with contents, in a very slow oven to bake for 6 hours.
- The fish is to be eaten cold.

Numbles Pie or Vagabond's Venison
(Bennington, Vermont — 1775)

Baked into a pie, with potatoes, turnips and squash, this was known as Numble Pie in Colonial Days — thus the expression, "He's eating Humble Pie."

- 1 heart of the deer (cut into bite sizes)
- Tongue of the deer (cut into bite sizes)
- 1 tablespoon of pork fat
- 2 onions, sliced
- mushroom caps in brine
- 2 tablespoons dark rum
- 2 tablespoons sherry
- 1/2 teaspoon paprika

Saute Onions with heart and tongue and stir for one minute. Add other ingredients and cover over medium heat for 30 minutes, then reduce heat and cook slowly for two hours.

Pigeon Stew
(Boston, Mass. — 1700s)

- 4 pigeons, feathered, boned, and cleaned
- 4 tablespoons of butter
- 4 cups of chicken gravy
- 1 onion, chopped
- 1 cup pickled mushrooms
- 1/2 cup of wine (dry)
- 1/2 teaspoon salt and pepper
- 1/2 teaspoon diced lemon peel
- 1/2 teaspoon ground clove
- 1/2 teaspoon mace
- 1/2 teaspoon marjoram
- 1/2 teaspoon bayleaf

Mix all into balls of butter and sew into the chest cavities of the birds. Roast uncovered 20 minutes at 325 degrees, then cover and cook for two hours.

Rare Old New England Recipes

Halibut Steaks
(Gloucester, Mass. — 1852)

- 4 half-pound halibut steaks
- 1/2 cup melted butter
- 2 tablespoons wine vinegar
- 3 tablespoons lemon juice
- 1 clove garlic, minced

- 1/4 teaspoon dry mustard
- 1/4 teaspoon each thyme and tarragon
- a few drops of hot pepper sauce
- 1/2 teaspoon salt
- 1/4 teaspoon pepper

Pour ingredients over fish and coat both sides. Bake in 450 degree oven for 12 minutes. The fish will flake when done. Serves 3 to 4 people.

Lobster Bisque or Mayhew's Marvelous Mixture
(Martha's Vineyard, Mass. — 1700s)

Gregory Mayhew, whose ancestors first settled and owned Martha's Vineyard Island, had this recipe, with but a few revisions, handed down to him from many generations, and he passed it on to me.

Mix all the following and heat just to boiling point, but do not boil. Serves six.

- only 1 lobster, cut into bite-sized chunks
- 1 can of crabmeat
- 1 can of green pea soup

- 2 cans evaporated milk
- 1 can tomato soup
- 1 small bottle of dry sherry wine.

Election Day Beef Stew
(Mayor Bill Ryan, Haverhill, Mass.)

- 1 1/2 stew beef, cut up
- 3 qts. of water
- 2 stalks of celery, cut up
- 3 carrots, cut up
- 3 large potatoes, cut up
- 1 lb. of tomatoes, skinned

- 3 beef bouillon cubes, or gravy
- 1 large onion
- flour
- salt and pepper
- 2 tablespoons of oil

Heat the oil in a four-quart pan. Then cut up the stew meat and coat it with flour. Throw the meat in the heated pan, adding all the ingredients except the carrots and potatoes. Simmer for two hours before proceeding to add the carrots. After adding carrots, simmer an additional 15 minutes before adding the potatoes. Now simmer until the potatoes are soft.

VI
Old Salts and the Pepper Trade

The first Europeans came to these shores to explore, fish, and trade with the Indians. Although a colony of English men and women attempted to settle in Maine in 1607, one long cold winter here was enough to send most of them scurrying back to their homeland. They did, however, manage to build the first American vessel to be used for commercial purposes, on the banks of the Kennebec River. She was 30-feet long, carried 30-tons of merchandise, and was christened **VIRGINIA**. On her maiden voyage, her cargo was fish, salt and furs, and she sailed from Maine to the Chesapeake Bay and thence to Plymouth, England. Also aboard were the majority of first settlers who had had enough of roughing it in New England. It was 23 years before another trading vessel was built here, and she was named **BLESSING OF THE BAY**, built and launched at Medford, Massachusetts on the Mystic River. She was a great success, plying the coast in swapping foodstuff and merchandise with the Dutch of New York. The third born and bred New England trader was the 200-ton **TRIAL**, built in Boston. As Governor Winthrop tells us in his journal, she *"took a loading of fish to Bilboa in 1643, that were sold at good profit. From thence she took freight to Malaga, and brought home wine, oil, fruit and iron..."* With the success of the **TRIAL**, shipbuilding of commercial vessels began to boom in the Bay Colony. In order to obtain desired and often needed items of trade from other ports-of-call, New England farmers and even housewives were encouraged by sea captains and ship owners to supply various foods, besides fish and meat, as cargo in order to make all sea voyages lucrative. The greatest problem was the spoilage of foods while in passage from one port to another, which prompted Anna King, a sea captain's daughter from Fairhaven, to write in her Journal, *"Potatoes and onions are the only vegetables that will keep on a long voyage, and there must be a large stock of them, but they did not go on board until just before the ship left the wharf."* Another sea captain's daughter named Schaw, from New Haven, Connecticut, writes in her journal that aboard her father's ship was a cargo of, *"a neck of beef, barrels of New England pork, oatmeal, stinking herring and potatoes that were excellent."*

Although onions and potatoes eventually proved to be a valuable export for New Englanders, both had a difficult time being accepted as a food here. The noted doctor in England at the time America was first being settled, was Nicholas Culpepper. In his 1653 *"Herbal's Book,"* he wrote that *"Onions are extremely hurtful...they breed but little nourishment, and that little is naught; they are bad meat, yet good physick for flegmatick people, they are opening and provoke urine; Roasted and applied they help boils and aposthumes, and they cure the bitings of mad dogs.* " If this weren't enough to eliminate onions from the daily diet, Culpepper assured housewives that, *"Onions ordinarily eaten cause headache, spoil the sight, dull the senses and fill the body full of wind."* Of the latter incrimination there may be some justification, but where his other conclusions came from is not known.

Apparently his well-read book came too late to fully influence the first Puritans, because at Salem in 1635, William Wood writes, *"This country aboundeth naturally with store of roots of great variety and good to eat...leeks and onions are ordinary."* Onions, in fact, were soon in such demand around the world that Salem sea captains prompted local farmers to move into the wilderness, clear the land, and grow onions as a crop for export to foreign lands. One who followed their advise was Daniel Rea in 1650, building a house and farm that stands to this day at Danvers, known then as Salem Farms. The Danvers farmers grew such plump tasty onions, and in such quantity, that Danvers, Massachusetts is still known as *"Onion Town."*

Like onions, which were often used in a plaster as a cure for lung infections, potatoes were rubbed on joints as a cure for arthritis. These little tubers, originally grown in the Andes Mountains by American Indians as food, were thought by most Europeans to cause tuberculosis and leprosy. The Incas called them *"Papas,"* and the Spanish introduced them as food to Europe in 1550, calling them *"Patatas."* Although the French, English and Scots initially considered them poisonous, the Irish planted them and ate them, and as we now know, potatoes flourished in Ireland, the name of the vegetable almost becoming synonymous with the Irish. When the Irish and Scotch-Irish settled in and around Londonderry, New Hampshire in 1719, the potato became popular and also was considered wonderful crop for export by merchant mariners because of its preservative powers. The New Englanders who were settled in when the Irish arrived, didn't immediately accept the potato as food, still believing it was bad for the health. The Reverend Edward Parker in his *"History of Londonderry,"* tells a story of another problem New England farmers had with the *"Irish Potato"* — they didn't know how to farm it. Londonderry settlers gave farmers of Andover, Massachusetts some of the potato seeds they had brought from Ireland. *"The potatoes were accordingly planted,"* Parker tells us, *"and they came up and flourished well; blossomed and produced balls, which the family supposed were the fruit to be eaten. They cooked the balls in various ways, but could not make them palatable, and pronounced them unfit for food. The next Spring, while ploughing their garden, the plough passed through where the potatoes had grown, and turned out some of great size, by which means they discovered their mistake."*

Various spices and herbs, although not available in large quantities here, were in constant demand for export to foreign communities by merchants and sea captains. As early as 1634, William Wood tells us that, *"the ground here affords us very good kitchen gardens for turnips, parsnips, carrots, radishes, pumpkins, cucumbers and onion,"* but he adds that, *"all manner of herbs for meat and medicine are yielded to man in the wilderness."* Turnip root was not only consumed as a food, but also eaten to quell fever, and it was often taken aboard vessels for the sake of keeping sailors hail and hardy. Ginger was also aboard almost every ship as a medicine for seasickness. Elecampane-root, growing wild in the pastures of New England was not only a popular condiment but also a medicine taken to alleviate many ills, including heart pain. New England mariners discovered that the Chinese craved Ginseng-root as a curative herb and aphrodisiac; they also often added it to their soups. Knowing that it grew wild in the woods of New England, locals here were hired to gather it. Ginseng brought in millions of dollars for Yankee traders and is still a 47 million dollar export from America to the Orient.

Even foods like parsley, for the flavoring of soups, and pumpkins were exported, but not taken on long voyages because of spoilage. Other vegetables we know today, like spinach — of which Doctor Culpepper said, *"I never read any physical virtues of it,"* — or celery, were either not grown or exported in the early days or were just not known by the Colonials. *"Sellery,"* was, in fact, considered quite a remarkable food when it appeared on the New England scene. Juliana Smith of St. Johnsbury, Vermont tells us that in November of 1776, *"Uncle Simeon had imported the seede from England just before the War began and only this year was there enough for table use, and you can eat it without cooking. It has to be taken up, roots and all, and buried in earth in the cellar through the winter and only pulling up some when you want to use it...Next year Uncle Simeon says he will be able to raise enough to give us all some."*

Vegetables like squash, the seeds of which the first settlers brought with them from England, was also being grown in gardens by the New England Indians; it quickly became a favored food here. Reverend Higginson of Salem wrote, *"Squash and pumpkins grow exceedingly well here, better than in England."* Squash, however, was preferred over pumpkin, and farmer Nicholas Pinion of Saugus, Massachusetts was arrested in 1649 for mistaking pumpkin seeds for squash seeds. He was actually taken to court and fined for swearing on Sunday; when he saw that pumpkins, and not squash, were growing in his garden, he cursed his mistake loudly enough for others to hear, others who quickly reported him to the constable and local minister. Saugus citizens believe that it is from Nicholas Pinion that we coined the phrase, *"He's a Pumpkin Head,"* but the people of New Haven, Connecticut believe this derogatory saying originated with them, when in the 17th century an ordinance was passed there, *"that all men and boys must have his hair cut round by his cap, and if he have no cap, then a pumpkin shell is to be propped on his head and hair cut round it."* Neither Pilgrims nor Puritans wanted anyone with long hair in their communities, and thus, if you didn't own a hat when you had your hair cut, you were called a *"Pumpkin Head."*

Almost all spices consumed were imported from the tropics, but most herbs used in Colonial Days came from New England. Fennel, Dill and Caraway were so common here that they were dubbed *"meeting seeds,"* as almost everyone nibbled on one or the other during the long Sunday sermons, *"to keep one from sleep, hiccupping or coughing."* Cinnamon, although superstition was that it came from mountain birdnests, was taken from the bark of the laurel trees, and always in demand, as were nutmeg, clove and saffron, which were consumed as condiments and medicines. Most herbs were grown in individual gardens by New England's pioneer women, some of whom got in trouble, especially at Salem in 1692, when they would use herbs to cure the sick and thus were thought to have witch powers, which led them to the gallows.

In 1810, Jonathan Lambert of Salem, known as a *"Yankee pirate,"* brought seeds and plants of the most desired foods and herbs to the Island of Tristan da Cunha in the South Atlantic, off the southern tip of South America. He and his men planted sugarcane, coffee trees, potatoes, onions, squash, turnips and many herbs, hoping that vessels would stop at the island to take on fresh food before they rounded the Horn into the Pacific Ocean. The idea was good and many vessels did stop, not only to feed the crew but to take on fresh fish and vegetables for export. Lambert, however, being leader of the farmers on this lonely island, decided he would become their Emperor and lord it over the few residents. When British marines landed at Tristan in 1816, however, they found the gardens grown over with weeds and only one man, Tomaasa Corrie, still living there. Corrie told the British commander that all the other farmers, including Lambert, had drowned in a fishing accident, but many then and now believe that Corrie, known more as a pirate than a farmer, murdered Lambert and the few farmers of Tristan and buried them all in their own gardens.

Good fresh food was not available and not expected by sailors who volunteered as crewmen aboard merchant sailing vessels. Life was tough at sea then, and the food was tough too, as a crewman aboard the merchant ship **RESOLUTION** explains, with possible slight exaggeration, *"The biscuits are so hard that we often use cannon balls to break them into pieces, and there are so many worms that we just eat them too. The salt-beef is hardened to the consistency of leather, sometimes used to carve scrimshaw. The water we drink is bad, with thick-fingered long fibers in it, giving it a glutinous consistency. There is scurvy on board which loosens the teeth and swells the limbs with a pain that will kill you."*

Biscuits, or what we call 'crackers,' were the mainstay of life at sea. They were made with flour and water, baked and dried, and hardly ever spoiled, but as the crewman above laments, they did get quite hard during long voyages. These *"ship's biscuits,"* as they were often called, could remain edible for over 50 years. To make them palatable, sailors often added water to them in a bowl to make a soup or gruel, a forerunner to what we know today as cereal. In the late 1700s, Timothy Dwight tells us that, *"Biscuits, dry and hard, but agreeable to the taste, are inferior to crackers made in the New England countryside."* The first cracker bakery in America was at Newburyport, Massachusetts in 1794, where all crackers were hand-molded, but in 1840 a cracker-making machine was introduced to the marketplace, and the cracker-barrel found in every country store became the habitual place for the men to gather around to discuss politics. It is from this impromptu gathering that we get the saying, *"He scraped the bottom of the barrel."* It was about this same time that graham crackers were added to the American food diet. Sylvester Graham of Connecticut believed that Americans ate too much meat and potatoes, *"and when you eat bread,"* he said, *"eat only wheat bread with the germ and bran intact."* Bakers hated Graham, but his crackers were popular. Peanut Butter to go with the crackers didn't come along until sixty years later when a St. Louis doctor ground peanuts into a paste to feed invalids who needed protein. It was, however, Washington Carver who experimented with using peanut-butter for just about everything from soups and salads to bread and shampoo. It is strictly an American food; people from other countries just do not take to peanut-butter the way we Americans do. Those who dared taste it, complained that it stuck in their mouth and they found it hard to swallow. It's the seaweed added to peanut-butter that makes it easy for us Americans to get it down.

Seaweed pudding, or *"kelp-pudding,"* was a dish fed to mariners. Introduced by Irish seafarers, it was dried and sweetened with sugar from the West Indies, so that it preserved well aboard ships. Dried fruits were also used to make up various puddings aboard ship, and from the captain's *"munching drawer,"* where he kept special treats such as nuts and sweets, something called *"marvellous-pudding"* was often baked by the cook for the officers of the vessel. The crew sometimes complained of eating *"wind-*

pudding," which meant they were served no pudding at all. *"Puddings formed of rice, flour, maize, and sometimes of buck-wheat, very frequently consitute a part of every New England dinner,"* Timothy Dwight wrote, and Sarah Emory reveals that *"biscuit-pudding,"* was a favorite of Newburyport sailors. Sarah also mentions in her journal of the late 1700s, that John Adams, known as *"Reformation John,"* came to Essex, Massachusetts to preach Methodism. *"He shouted so loud,"* she says, *"that one could see the pudding he ate for dinner."* Although puddings, be they eaten on land or sea, are not as popular today, they have been replaced by another food, which, for all intensive purposes, is a pudding. Ferdinand Schumacher developed a fast-cooking oatmeal in America in 1850. Prior to this, oatmeal was eaten by horses only, not humans. Two years later, *"Airy Biscuits,"* also called *"Wheat Pillows,"* were introduced by health zealot John Kellogg. His brother, Bill Kellogg, argued with John about flaking and flattening wheat and corn, so he went off on his own to develop cornflakes which, with sugar added, became a popular breakfast food. Known as breakfast cereals today, they are just old, redesigned puddings in disguise.

Probably the two items in greatest demand by the colonists and seafarers alike, were pepper and mustard. In his *"Every Day Life In The Massachusetts Colony,"* noted historian George Francis Dow writes that, *"pepper and spice were used to a considerable extent,"* and that, *"mulled and spiced wines were drunk in the absence of tea and coffee, and highly-seasoned dishes were popular."* Ground mustard was made into a paste, much like the mustard we know today, using vinegar. However, it would soon go flat, so mustard powder, sprinkled on food like salt and pepper, was the rage in colonial times. Mustard powder was used extensively aboard ships to hide the taste of food gone rancid. Mixed with water, it was also applied externally to cure chest colds and rheumatism — thus came the popular expression, *"does it cut the mustard?"* In proper quantity it was also used, since ancient days, as a poison. The spoilage of mustard was always a fear prior to the mid-18th century, because it was believed that if it spoiled it would immediately become a poison, causing death to any partaker. This fear was tempered somewhat on September 19, 1752, when the *Boston Gazette* reported:

"Mustard Revived: Mustard Maker John Ingram of Lisbon Arrives; The Original Flower of Mustard Maker, John Ingram, now living at the House of Mrs. Townsend, near Oliver's Dock, Boston, prepares Flower of Mustard to such perfection, by a method unknown to any person but himself, that it retains its strength, flavour and colour seven years; being mix'd with hot or cold water, in a Minute's Time it makes the strongest Mustard ever eat, not the least bitter, yet of a delicate and delightful flavour, and gives a most surprising grateful taste to Beef, Pork, Lamb, Fish, Sallad, or

other Sauces. It is approved of by divers eminent Physicians as the only Remedy in the Universe in all nervous disorders, sweetens all Juices, and rectifies the whole mass of blood to admiration...Merchants and Captains of Ships shall have good allowance to sell again.''

Pepper, like mustard, was either sprinkled on food, or made into a sauce or paste to provide a tang and hot taste to various foods. Today it is used sparingly, but in old New England it was more coveted than salt as an additive to foods. Used externally in paste form, Colonials considered it a sure cure for the ever-present shingles. Although pepper comes in many forms and colors — even the chili and cayenne from Central America, the Spaniards called pepper — the most desired was that of the Indonesian Spice Islands. The Dutch and Portuguese competed to monopolize the pepper trade in the 1500s, and in the 1600s, England's East India Company controlled the Oriental pepper trade. In New England, prior to the Revolutionary War, pepper was purchased from the English at exhorbitant prices. One New Englander who joined the British East India Company and made a small fortune, much of it by defrauding his employer, was Elihu Yale. He had joined the company in 1672, and by the turn of the century, his old pal Cotton Mather, who was refused the job as President of Harvard College, went to him for money to start another prestigious college in New England. Thus, from a peck of pickled peppers, the *"Fighting Eli"* of Yale University originated.

It was after the Revolution that New England sea captains became true *"masters"* of their vessels. The many privateers built during the war were converted into merchant vessels, and the horizons for trade in foreign ports were unlimited, with no more interference from Mother England, whose taxes, fees, duties and monopoly on imported goods had driven Americans to ultimate defiance. New England's merchant mariners began trading with Russia, China, India, Africa, Arabia, Japan, South America and Australia. Great quantities of coffee, cocoa, tea, flour, olive oil, ginger, rice, wine, dates, figs, oranges, almonds, spices, including the first taste of Chinese food, arrived on our shores and filtered inland. New England ports quickly became the world market for the new America. The port of Salem, under the leadership of Elias Derby, seemed to produce the most daring of these maritime marketeers, her traders exploring deeper and deeper into foreign uncharted waters, her captains given wide latitude by ship-owners on where and what they might bargain for, and the crews given a large percentage of any profits made. Derby had many Salem competitors in the merchant trade, including his relatives by marriage, the Crowninshields, five of whom were brothers and sea captains, owning and operating their own fleet of merchant ships.

Even with this glut of foodstuffs coming into America, pepper remained hard to find in foreign ports, and therefore it was expensive for the common housewife to purchase. In England, pepper became so precious that the dock workers of London were made to sew their pockets shut so that they couldn't snitch any pepper while they were unloading vessels from the Indies. The ingenious and tenacious Derby was determined to find pepper at a reasonable price, so he sent out the brig **CADET,** commanded by Johathan Carnes, in April of 1788, on a mystery voyage, and the vessel disappeared for two years. When she returned, Carnes brought her into Boston instead of Salem, hoping that his discovery of Sumatra as a pepper paradise might not be revealed to Derby's Salem rivals. Because the families of the crewmen were anxious at not hearing from loved ones for so long, a *Salem Gazette* reporter got wind of her arrival and wrote the following in the May 18, 1790 edition:

"Captain Carnes, aboard the CADET, absent on an India voyage upwards to two years, arrived in Boston. The first American vessel to trade at Sumatra, Moco Paddang and other Chinese Ports never traded at before. She returns with Cassia, Pepper, Cinnamon, Camphor, and Gold dust."

The Crowninshield boys apparently didn't get the message and didn't connect Sumatra with pepper, so Derby's and Carnes' secret was safe. Carnes had found Sumatra, teeming with pepper plants, by mistake, and even his crew didn't know where they were when the pepper was loaded aboard. Carnes persuaded the natives to grow more and promised to return for all they could produce, and the price was cheap, enough to bring Derby a 700 percent profit. The next Derby ship to head for Sumatra was his **GRAND SACHEM,** but she wrecked off Bermuda, so he sent out the schooner **RAJAH,** 120-tons, again under command of Jonathan Carnes. She too vanished for almost two years, her whereabouts unknown but to Derby. When she returned to Salem she was packed with pepper, and again, Derby made $700.00 on every dollar spent on the cargo. This, of course, now sparked the interest of the Crowninshield brothers and of other merchant mariners. Members of the **RAJAH** crew were wined and dined by the Crowninshields, but they couldn't actually say where they had been when they loaded the pepper, but they were sure that it was *"somewhere East of the Cape."* On the **RAJAH's** second voyage for pepper, the Crowninshields made sure that they had well-paid spies among the crew members. When the **RAJAH** returned from her second profitable voyage, the secret was out. The Crowninshields waited for the **RAJAH** to once more depart for Sumatra, then they sent out their 209-ton **BELISARIUS,** making the quickest run to Sumatra on record, returning to Salem, her hold filled with pepper, on July 18, 1801. The trade with Sumatra was then open to all, and Salem soon was known as *"The Pepper Capitol of The World,"* her merchants, like the British before them, holding a profitable monopoly on all pepper trade. This monopoly by Salem lasted until 1867, the Salem ship **TARQUIN,** being the last of the pepper traders to enter Sumatra that year and return home with cargo that turned a profit.

Salem Harbor was too shallow for the sleek clipper ships, which appeared on the scene about 1851. The world marketplace called for faster time between one port and another so that fresh food could be transported, and the *"clippers"* answered this demand. These 200-foot *"needle-bowed"* ships, carrying *"clouds of billowing canvas,"* could quickly out-distance any bark, brigantine, schooner or ship in the maritime trade. The great **FLYING CLOUD,** built in Boston by Donald McKay, sailed from New York to San Francisco in 1854 with full cargo, including fresh eggs and passengers, in 89 days, a speed record that remained unbroken until 1989. Ironically, her captain was a Salem boy, Josiah Cressy. Cressy, who had sailed every kind of vessel since 1826, also lived to see the demise of clipper ships in 1861, when steam power began ruling land and sea in the transporting of goods. For almost 250 years, sailing ships not only transported immigrants, but also food and materials needed by our forefathers; later they transported, as well, the fruits of our harvest on to others. Our merchant mariners of old braved treacherous uncharted seas to feed this nation, and today we can only marvel at their courage and ingenuity at providing such variety and abundance.

The port of New Bedford, teeming with activity into the mid-1800s, began its decline before the century was over. Photo courtesy of The Dartmouth Society — New Bedford Whaling Museum, Massachusetts.

Rare Old New England Recipes

Onion Shortcake
(Vermont)

- 8 onions, sliced thin
- 1 pint of sour cream
- 1 egg, beaten into cream
- biscuit dough

Place biscuit dough in a baking dish. Sprinkle onions evenly throughout dish, adding salt and pepper. Pour the cream in mixed with the egg, and bake at 450 degrees for 15 minutes.

Scrapple
(New Hampshire)

- pork heart, kidneys, and shoulder meat cooked well and then grind.
- 3 lbs. of ground pork and innards
- 1 lb. of finely ground corn meal
- sage and nutmeg
- maple syrup

Place all in a pan with the juices of the meat. Add sage, nutmeg, salt and pepper while cooking. Stir well. Then let it cool and harden. Fry it and serve hot with a maple syrup topping.

Shanty Chowder
(Maine)

- 1/4 cup of melted butter
- 1/2 cup of finely minced onions
- 2 cups of chicken stock
- 1 cup chopped celery
- 1 cup thinly sliced carrots
- 1 lb. of fish fillets (any fish will do)
- 3 cups of milk
- 1 cup light cream
- 1 cup crabmeat
- 1/4 cup flour
- 1 can of minced clams

Make a paste of the milk and flour after cooking all other ingredients in a pan for 20 minutes. Add the paste and stir up well until thick and let sit for a day.

Cranberry Pudding
(Cape Cod)

- 2 egg yolks, beaten lightly
- 1 cup of sugar
- 1/2 cup of milk
- 3 tablespoons melted butter
- 2 cups of cranberries
- 1 1/2 cups flour
- 1 teaspoon cream of tartar
- 3/4 teaspoon soda

Mix and bake all for 45 minutes in a 350 degree oven.

Rare Old New England Recipes

Green Pepper Relish
(Massachusetts)

- 8 green peppers (remove seeds and then grind or pulverize)
- 2 red peppers (remove seeds and then grind or pulverize)
- 6 1/2 cups sugar
- 1 1/2 cups vinegar
- 1 bottle of Certo

Mix peppers and place in two cups, add vinegar and sugar, mix well, and bring to a boil for 2 minutes. Take off fire and add Certo. Stir for 8 Minutes, let cool and bottle or use.

Sweet Potato Pudding
(Connecticut)

- 2 cups of grated, raw sweet potatoes
- 1 cup milk
- 1/4 cup melted butter
- 2 teaspoons lemon juice
- 2 eggs beaten fine
- 1/2 teaspoon cinnamon
- 1 pinch of nutmeg

Mix potatoes and eggs in separate bowls and stir in one cup of sugar, then add the other ingredients and mix well. Pour all into a greased pan and bake at 350 degrees for 30 minutes.

Shredded Wheat Pudding
(Rhode Island)

- 2 shredded wheat biscuits
- 2 eggs, beat lightly
- 2 cups milk
- 3/4 cup molasses
- 1 teaspoon cinnamon
- 1/4 teaspoon salt

Pour mix over the biscuits, adding a teaspoon of butter, then bake for 45 minutes at 350 degrees. Serve with whipped cream topping.

Pumpkin Puddin' Pie
(Vermont)

- 1 cup strained pumpkin
- 1 cup milk
- 2 tablespoons evaporated milk
- 3 eggs, lightly beaten
- 1/2 cup sugar
- 1 teaspoon cinnamon
- 1/2 teaspoon nutmeg
- 1/4 teaspoon each of cloves, ginger, and salt

Pour all into a pie shell and bake for 10 minutes at 325 degrees.

Bob Cahill at Salem Willows, with E.W. Hobbs ice cream, popcorn and candy pavilion to his right. Active for over 100 years, it was here that ice cream cones were introduced in 1885. At right is a New Bedford refreshment pavilion of 1875. Photo by T.E. White. Courtesy of The Society Of The Preservation Of New England Antiquities, Boston, MA.

The Boston Tea Party, 1773, and Boston's Steaming Teapot, 1873. Painting Courtesy of the John Hancock Insurance Co, Boston

VII
Candy, Coffee, And The Creature

As conservative and righteous as America's first Pilgrim and Puritan settlers were, they craved sweets and enjoyed various stimulants such as coffee and tea as much as their 20th century counterparts. They also adored beer, ale and wine and consumed these daily if available. When the hermit Blackstone invited Governor Winthrop and his Puritan followers to cross the river from Charlestown to Boston in July of 1630 because there was *"a lack of pure water"* at Charlestown, Winthrop's group obliged Blackstone by settling in Boston. Governor Winthrop commented that, *"There is good water to drink here, till wine and beer can be made."* When ingredients were at hand, beer and ale were brewed in every home each week, and even infants were given beer and wine instead of milk to drink — milk was only for newborns. Once the meeting-house was built, which also doubled as a church, the second order of business for the residents of every new American community was to build a pub or tavern, which the Pilgrims and Puritans called *"ordinaries."* So important were these public places of drinking to the new settlers that in 1656 the Massachusetts General Court passed a law that, *"all villages and townes are liable to a fine for not sustaining an ordinary."* A few years later, the leading Puritan minister of the day, Cotton Mather, cried from the pulpit that, *"every other house in Boston is an ale house."*

Besides such beverages produced from their own crops, strong drinks such as rum, brandy and whiskey were consumed in vast quantities in the early days. Apothecary William Woodcocke of Salem was licensed on March 25, 1662, *"to still strange water and sell it at retail."* Apple-jack, hard cider, brandy and wine were made from America's first fruits, and whiskey was often the final product of corn and potatoes. These were basically the *"strong drink,"* and *"strange water,"* referred to in Pilgrim and Puritan writings, but the culprit that desecrated the New England Indians and ruined many a white settler, was that thick, brown and ever sweet demon-rum, better known to our ancestors as *"The Creature."* John Dunton of England, visiting New England in 1686, wrote home about rum drinking Bostonians, stating that, *"there are several of them so addicted to it, that they begin to doubt whether it be a sin or not, and seldom go to bed without muddy brains..."*

It was from the sugarcane of the West Indies that molasses, the main ingredient of rum, was produced, but it was here in New England that rum was perfected into the smooth, sweet liquid desired by so many. Boston, Medford, Salem and Newport, Rhode Island provided the main distilleries, beginning in the early 1700s. As early as 1694, Newport was noted and later criticized for its merry-go-round trade of *"having over 120 vessels carrying about 100 slaves per voyage from Africa to the West Indies, where they were traded for molasses, which was shipped back to Newport to make rum, which in turn was sold to procure more slaves.''* By the year 1810, there were over 14,000 American distilleries producing some 25 million gallons of rum per year. It was not just consumed in the pubs, taverns and inns, but as a daily ration aboard fishing, trading and naval vessels. It was a panacea for doctors, often given to infants to quell their cries; mixed with *"nine drops of beeswax,''* it was considered the cure for the common cold. Added to tea, rum was even praised for calming frayed nerves. Housewives used it not too sparingly in fruit-cakes, puddings and pies, and it was often added to warm milk for children and the aged on wintery nights before they entered their cold rooms.

A hard-to-swallow, large spoonful of molasses was given to every child when spring appeared, as was a mouthful of cod-liver oil. *"It gets your blood flowing for the active months ahead,''* was my mother's reason for the annual ritual. This was a must in every New England home from the early 1700s to the mid 20th century. *"It's full of iron,''* was another of her coaxes when I tried to resist. The advent of molasses in quantity increased the number and variety of sweets available to New Englanders, especially to those living along the seacoast. Until about the mid-1800s, sugar was a luxury and almost unaffordable, selling at $2.65 per pound in 1742 and climbing to over $200.00 per bag during the Revolutionary War. Many New England farmers kept beehives to acquire honey on a regular basis, and collecting maple sugar from the trees was a thriving activity, but it was never available in vast quantities. Molasses became an easy substitute for such costly sweeteners when the West Indian ports were open for trade with New Englanders. Tea and coffee, served with a spoonful of molasses , became a common drink in seacoast households in the 18th century, and a new sweet sensation which got its name from the Persian word *"kand,''* meaning sugar, began appearing in various sweet-shops. By the early 1800s, Boston was known as *"The Sugar Capitol Of America,''* and her step-sister, Salem, was heralded as *"The Candy Capitol.''* Travelling through Boston in 1808, Edward Augustus Kendall noted another unusual use for the sticky substance molasses. He writes in his journal entitled *"Travels Through Northern Parts Of The United States,''* that, *"the bricks which visitors admired were of red color, while those of an older period were brown... and as the humidity, together with frosts, tended to disintegrate them, an attempt had been made to render them impenetrable by saturation with molasses.''*

The first candy factory, started by James Boies and John Hanon, was located in Dorchester, Massachusetts in 1765, but Hanon left Boston for Ireland ten years later, never to return. Unfortunately, he had been one of the few to join the British forces when the Colonies were demanding their independence. In 1806, Salem had its first candy company which made lemon and peppermint twists wrapped in paper as well as multi-flavored candy-sticks called *"blackjacks."* Some 19 years later, a destitute woman of nobility was banished from England due to *"an indiscretion"* and, with her son, she fled to America and settled in Salem. Within a few months she began creating new kinds of candy and began selling them in the streets and door-to-door from a one-horse wagon. She was known as Madame Spencer and her jawbreakers were called *"gibraltars"* due to their resemblance to white rock, and are still a popular treat in Salem today. Another hard candy conceived by Madame Spencer were her *"zanzibars"*; Salem sea captains were convinced to carry such unique sweets to other countries in vast quantities, where they were also soon in high demand. Not surprisingly, Madame Spencer became a wealthy woman and chose to return to her native England where her son later became a distinguished British knight, Sir Thomas Spencer. It is said that, for over fifty years, no vessel would leave Salem without a case of gibraltar candies to trade in India, Africa, or China. Even noted poet Charles Timothy Brooks of Newport wrote in 1853:

> *"Does the old green Gibraltar cart still stop*
> *Up in old Paved Street at Aunt Hannah's Shop?*
> *Beside Cold Spring drop the sweet acorns still?*
> *Do boys dig flagroot now beneath Legge's Hill?..."*

So, for her short stay in America, Madame Spencer surely made her distinguished mark in the history books, and left America behind with a few cavities, a new sweet-tooth, and undoubtably a few broken ones from chomping on gibralters.

At sea, hard candies were chomped and sucked as sails were hauled and furled, and an old favorite of sailors was a sweet known as *"dandy-funk"* made of water, molasses, and bits of hard-tack. Although only hard candy was exported from New England to such places as the tropics, it was the tropics that provided the world with that scarce but ever-desirable sweet — chocolate. It was Christopher Columbus who discovered chocolate in the New World, but he didn't understand what a treasure he had stumbled upon. Columbus had, however, introduced sugar-cane plants to the West Indies on his second voyage — his mother-in-law owned an extensive sugar-cane plantation in Spain — and these plants thrived on the tropical islands. The Aztec Indians drank *"chocolatl"* as a gift from the gods and used the *"cacao bean"* as currency. The great chief Montezuma drank fifty cups of chocolate a day. It is even recorded that the Commander of the Spaniards, Hernan Cortez, was welcomed by the Indians with a golden cup of chocolate when he and his men arrived in Mexico. Cortez realized the value of chocolate immediately, as well as another drinkable substance, *"tlixochitl,"* or vanilla as we know it, also consumed by the Indians. Mixed with Columbus' sugar-cane, the two delicacies became as valuable as gold in Spain. In fact, so precious was chocolate to the Spaniards that, for over 100 years, they managed to hide its source from other Europeans. The Dutch, French, and English finally sent spies to Mexico to uncover the mystery. Thus it wasn't until after the Pilgrims had landed at Plymouth that chocolate and vanilla found their way into English society. James Boies sold chocolate from his factory in Dorchester in 1765, and the Boston Gazette of September 5-12, 1737, reads: *"Chocolate Mill at Salem — By a Gentleman of the Town this day, brought to perfection, an Engine to grind Cocoa. It is a contrivance that cost much less than any commonly used, and will effect all that which the chocolate Grinders do with their Mills and Stones...and the chocolate made by it is finer and better, and there is little or no need of fire in the making..."*

With the availability of chocolate came new treats for the Colonials: chocolate cake, cookies, puddings, milk, and the ever-popular hot-cocoa mix — steeping hot with milk or water, it came close to replacing coffee and tea as the favored drink and quickly became the favorite of children. A nearly miraculous event occurred at Franklin, Massachusetts concerning chocolate in February of 1890. In the midst of an evening storm, word passed from house to house that it was snowing chocolate candy. Many children, lanterns in hand, went out into the storm to investigate and discovered snowbanks near the railroad tracks heaped with little mounds of chocolate. Soon there were hundreds of children and adults digging into the snow with mittened hands and shovels. They excitedly scooped up the delicacies into boxes, baskets and pockets. When the sun rose the following morning, neighboring villagers joined in the hunt, reaching into the snow and coming up with fistfuls of chocolate candies until the snow itself started to take on a chocolate hue. A train, it was later discovered, had derailed in the night, and a freight car filled with chocolates had tipped on its side, spilling chocolate for almost a half-mile down the length of the tracks. To this day it is remembered in Franklin as *" the night the chocolate train came to town."*

The chocolate candy bar as we know it today was created in 1911, just in time to provide American doughboys with quick energy food in the trenches during World War I, but chocolate ice cream was already available nearly 150 years earlier. History reveals that George Washington was addicted to ice cream, especially chocolate-flavoured, and it is recorded that he consumed $200.00 worth in the year 1790 alone. President James Madison's wife, Dolly, also had a constant yen for ice cream, but she was partial to strawberry. How ice cream truly originated is lost to history, but, like the frozen chocolates of Franklin, the milk and honey so often mentioned in works of Biblical times were probably inadvertently left out in the cold one night, and ice cream was born. The hand-cranked ice cream maker, which allowed families to easily make their own homemade frozen favorites, was invented by American Nancy Johnson in 1846. The first ice cream cones in New England were created by E.W. Hobbs at Salem Willows in Massachusetts in 1885. In 1882, the same Mr. Everett Hobbs started America's first popcorn company, The National Popcorn Works, in Lynn, Massachusetts. E.W. Hobbs & Company is still doing business in their original seaside home at Salem Willows Park, making ice cream, popcorn,and saltwater taffy using much of the same machinery they started with over 100 years ago.

The sweet smell and sight of molasses being twisted and turned by ancient machines at Hobbs' at the Willows is one of my earliest and fondest recollections of youth, but on the waterfront in Boston on a hot sticky day, that sweet smell of molasses from days gone by is also in the air - but it reminds one only of a stomach-wrenching tragedy. It was high-noon of January 15, 1919, and exceptionally warm for a winter day in Boston. Towering above the hustle and bustle of seaside Commercial Street was a fifty-foot high metallic tank containing 2.2 million gallons of molasses. Without warning there was heard a loud roar as the tank collapsed, spewing out great thick waves of the gooey sugar in every direction — 14,000 tons of it. It engulfed everything and everyone in its path, first smothering 12 children who were playing in the street, then smashing into the firehouse, crushing a fireman to death. Five teamsters eating lunch in a shack by the water's edge were drowned in molasses when the great wave demolished the shack and moved on through the teamsters yard to swallow up all the horses and the wagons. One teamster named Glynn was picked up by the wave in his truck and rode the crest right into the water, where his truck sank and he drowned. A sheet of metal from the molasses tank slammed into the overhead elevated railway abutments, and it also collapsed only seconds after a train filled with passengers had gone by. An elderly woman was found hours later under the railway, covered with molasses and thought dead until she began crying. One teamster, still sitting in his wagon and holding onto the horses reigns, was uncovered two days later, looking like a statue, preserved in molasses, but dead. In all, thirty people lost their lives that day and some of the bodies were never found. It took months to clean up the mess, and those living in the North End of Boston refused to ever use molasses in preparing food or drink again. Some thought the tank had exploded because of fermenting molasses inside the tank or perhaps due to the warm temperature, but it was determined that the tank had been structurally weak and had never been inspected. Believe it or not, the smell of it lingers on even now on hot days, as does the heartache in a few Boston families.

Another sticky substance that has become synonymous with sweet treats, is chewing gum. It, too, comes to us from Central America, mainly from the sap of the sapodilla tree in Yucatan, Mexico. It didn't become popular in America until the mid-1800s. The great Santa Anna, general of the Mexican Army that attacked and defeated the Alamo in 1836, was an addicted gum chewer, and when he found asylum in New York, he befriended Tom Adams, who also became a gum chewer. Tom rolled it and flattened it and began adding various flavors to it. He even invented a gum-making machine. With added spearmint or peppermint and plenty of sugar, chewing gum became the rage of the early 20th century. Its popularity seems to be ebbing as the century comes to an end, only with the possible exception of bubblegum. It once was the most advertised product in America, thanks to a gum producer and promoter named William Wrigley.

Of course, if it weren't for sugar, many foods and popular drinks probably never would have been consumed at all. Even coffee and tea, although constantly desired since their discovery, would never have become such a part of the daily diet if it weren't for the added sugar, spooned out for every cup, to fit each individual's taste. Today sugar is seemingly valued, if erroneously, higher than all other edible substances. Just imagine America's most popular drink, Pepsi and Coke, without sugar or a sugar substitute — would we or our children drink it? Yet, sugar was first used as a stimulant prescribed by certified doctors who also advised its use as an external balm for wounds. The first soft drink, gingerale, came to America via Ireland in 1850, where it was concocted and bottled by a doctor name Cantrall. Canada Dry Gingerale was exported to New England in 1921. The carbonated soft drink as we know it today was the invention of a teenage girl in 1885. A *"soda-jerk"* in Virginia, the young inventor mixed some *"fizz-water"* with syrup of molasses for her boyfriend, and he liked it so much that they decided to name it for her pharmacist father, Doctor Pepper. The *"fizz-water"* was carbonated water, produced by Englishman Joseph Priestly in 1772 while he was trying to duplicate the ever-popular mineral water. All this was perfected by another pharmacist, John Pemberton of Atlanta, Georgia who combined carbonated water, syrup and a few other ingredients to make *"a new elixir for the nerves and for hangovers,"* and he called it Coca Cola. Molasses had now come 180 degrees, producing the rum that caused hangovers and the Coca Cola that supposedly cured them.

Coffee, like most soft drinks of the day, has always been high in caffeine. Discovered to be a stimulant as early as 850 A.D., it was thankfully consumed by Catholic monks in Africa to help them stay awake. The name comes from where the red coffee-beans were first located, Kaffa, Ethiopia, by a cow herder named Kaldi, who noticed his cows gained energy after chomping on the beans. He then ate one and liked the bitter taste, but couldn't sleep that night. By the 1300's coffee was made into a drink by crushing the beans, and widely consumed in Arab sheikdoms as a diuretic. The Dutch wanted coffee seeds, but the Arabs refused to part with their bitter brew, beans or seeds. The Dutch managed to steal seeds in 1690, and coffee became a European panacea. The Dutch persuaded the English and French that a cup of coffee would cure just about any illness, including smallpox. Smallpox was very prevalent in New England in the early years, so coffee was in constant demand. When sugar was added to the cup to curb the bitter taste, it was realized that they went hand-in-glove, and when the British became heavy-handed with their tea tax on the Colonials, coffee replaced tea as the morning stimulant. In 1802, an English visitor to New England wrote, *"a breakfast among the inhabitants, and even among the poorest, for there are none which may be called really poor, consists of tea or coffee, brown bread with butter, salt of fresh fish, fried or broiled."* It was a Massachusetts schoolboy, Hanson Gregory, who provided the perfect mate for a good cup of coffee in the early 1900s, when he told his mother to cut a hole in the center of her little dough-cakes before she fried them, so he could hold them better while he ate them and not get sugar all over himself; she complied. The other kids at school, after seeing Hanson's new treat, asked their mothers to do the same, and the doughnut was born.

The most widely consumed liquid in the world is obviously water, though tea comes in as a close second everywhere but in America, thanks to Boston's famous tea party. Tea, like so many other delicious foods and drinks, was discovered by accident many centuries ago. The Chinese Emperor Shen Nung was boiling water in 2737 B.C., so the story goes, to purify it before drinking, and the leaves from a nearby bush fell into the water. Shen Nung liked the sweet aroma it produced, and believing the gods had placed the leave in the water on purpose, he drank the concoction produced, and thus tea was born. Though soon becoming the favored drink of the Chinese and Japanese, tea leaves didn't make it West in quantity until the Dutch began exporting it in 1610. Surprisingly, the great tea-consuming British weren't able to introduce the beverage to their country until 1650 due to a Dutch monopoly, but soon it was sold in almost every street corner shop in London. Britain's East India Company had a monopoly on tea export until after the Revolutionary War, and it was the vessels of Elias Derby of Salem that circumvented British barriers in the Far East and brought home the tea directly to America.

The famous Tea Party in Boston, December 1773, was not the first act of defiance in New England against a tea tax imposed on Colonials. In 1689, some 700 women marched on the bake shop of James Bowler in Lynn, Massachusetts, seizing and destroying his supply of tea. Bowler was not only charging too much for his tea, thought the women of Lynn, but was hoarding it. At the Boston Tea Party, where some 200 patriots dressed like Indians disposed of three entire shiploads of tea into the harbor, it was ordered that if any patriot was caught taking even a pinch of tea for himself, he was to be severely punished. One disguised Indian named Conner did attempt to steal some of the tea for his wife, but as fellow Mohawk George Hewes tells us, *"he was detected. He had ript up the lining of his coat under the arms, and had nearly filled 'em with tea...We not only stripped him of his clothes, but gave him a coat of mud, with a severe beating into the bargain."* With such treatment of British tea drinkers before the Revolution even began, it's no wonder that Americans lost their taste for tea.

It is interesting to note, however, that one boy named Henry Purkett, who was helping the men dispose of the tea from the three docked British ships that night, stumbled home and fell into his bed exhausted, but in the morning his mother found mounds of tea gathered in his discarded clothes. She scooped it up and collected it into a bottle, and her descendants retain the tea from that historic day to this.

There was another tea party in Boston, 102 years after the original one that preceded the Revolution. This party, however, held on New Year's Day in 1875, centered around a controversial copper tea kettle, known to New Englanders as the giant *"Golden Teapot."* For the Tea Party Centennial, the owners of Boston's Oriental Tea Company hired coppersmiths E.B. Badger and John Strang to build a large teapot that they could hang over the door of their tea company, located at Scully Square. Completed in 14 days, the kettle was mounted with a steampipe connected to its spout so that it always appeared brewing. It immediately became an object of interest and curiosity, but no one, not even the builders, knew how big it was or how much liquid it could hold. To answer these questions, a contest was initiated, and the person who could guess the kettle's capacity was to win a 40 lb. chest of the company's best tea. There were 12,571 guesses, varying from ten gallons to 3,700 gallons — obviously the giant kettle was very deceiving. About 20,000 people showed up at noon on a cold New Year's Day to appease their curiosity. To the surprise of everyone, before the measuring began, the cap on the kettle popped off, and eight boys climbed out of the kettle and escaped down a ladder, one by one; they had been hiding in the kettle since early morning. To the crowd's further surprise, a six-foot man climbed out after them. The capacity of the kettle was then carefully measured by filling it with water, taking nearly an hour to fill it to the brim. It held, and still holds, 227 gallons, two quarts and one pint. An engineer won, his guess being only three gallons off. In April of 1967, the Boston Globe headlined, *"Boston's golden, ever steaming tea kettle, a landmark which ranks with such Hub attractions as the swan boats on the Public Garden, the gold dome of the State House and even Bunker Hill Monument, is going to be moved."* Scully Square was being leveled for a new Government Center, and historians were up in arms in opposition over the moving of the kettle. It was, however, finally moved only thirty feet from its original perch. It still continues to let off steam today, next to city hall in downtown Boston. New England natives often choose to meet at the spot when they're on a shopping spree, and tourists can still always be found gawking up at its coppery mass in amazement. The ancient kettle has been labeled by the Society of the Preservation of Antiquities as *"the oldest original animated trade sign in the United States,"* and it is still beloved by Bostonians. And, if not for an incident about a mile down the street, at dockside about 220 years ago, the ingredients that the kettle so diligently keeps brewing, might have been loved by the majority of Bostonians too, but then, what would we do without our daily spot of coffee, and one of Hanson's cakes with the hole in the middle.

As of late, many good old American foods and drinks have been criticized for one thing or another — too much cholesterol, too much fat, not enough bran or fiber, too spicy, too bland — the list of complaints goes on and on. What's good for us one day seems to be bad the next, and visa-versa. Although Americans may be the fussiest eaters and the most well-fed people on earth, the toil, determination, experimentation and ingenuity of our forefathers have provided us with a land of plenty. We are healthier and bigger-in-stature than our world counterparts, because we are so well-fed. The quantity, quality and variety of our food and drink is not just due to those Colonial farmers and fishermen, but to the live *"ingredients"* hailing from many foreign lands, who are constantly being added to America's melting pot. They have created and will continue to create new dishes for our daily diet. Throughout American history, immigrants have continued to provide new foods and new ways of preparing foods, constantly enhancing what we eat — so, keep the new dishes coming. But, a special thanks to the first New Englanders who first prepared our abundant tables — for they provided us with the sugar and spice of life.

Rare Old New England Recipes

Jelly Squares
(Freedom Acres, Wilmot, New Hampshire)

- 1 cup of jelly
- 2 cups of flour
- 1/4 teaspoon of soda
- 1 teaspoon of baking powder
- 1 cup of brown sugar
- 1 cup of white sugar
- 3 eggs
- Vanilla and salt

Mix wet ingredients with beater, then mix in dry ingredients. Spread evenly on 17″ by 11″ cookie sheet. Mix in jelly until all lumps are out, spread evenly on top. Bake for 25 minutes at 325 degrees. When cool, cut into squares.

Ginger Cream Candy
(Grand Turk, Salem, Mass.)

- 2 cups of white sugar
- 1 cup of brown sugar
- 3/4 cup of milk
- 2 tablespoons of corn syrup (boil at 270 degrees to soft thickness)
- 2 tablespoons of butter
- 2 tablespoons of crystallized ginger, do not stir.

Cool mix to luke warm and add a teaspoon of vanilla. Beat contents until creamy and pour into buttered pan, when cold, cut into squares.

Whiskey Cake
(Cork & Kerry, Haverhill, Mass.)

- 1/4 cup of rye whiskey
- 1 cup of walnuts, chopped
- 1 box of vanilla instant pudding
- 1 box of white cake mix
- 3/4 cup of milk
- 4 eggs beaten a little
- 1/2 cup of oil

Topping
- 1/4 cup of butter
- 3/4 cup of sugar
- 1/4 cup of rye whiskey

Mix all, bake at 350 degrees for 1 hour. Topping: bring mixed ingredients to a boil for five minutes. Pour hot topping over cake and allow to stand for 30 minutes before eating.

Rare Old New England Recipes

Old Molasses Sponge Cake

- 1/2 cup molasses
- 1/2 cup sugar
- 1/2 cup shortening
- 1 egg
- 1 cup hot water

- 2 cups flour
- 1 tablespoon of soda
- 1/2 teaspoon ginger
- 1/2 teaspoon cloves
- 1/4 teaspoon nutmeg

Mix and bake for 30 minutes in medium oven — til cake pulls away from the pan.

Molasses Cookies

- 3/4 cup of fat
- 1 cup sugar
- 1 egg
- 4 tablespoons molasses

- 2 teaspoons soda
- 1 teaspoon ginger
- 2 cups sifted flour

Roll batter into small ball sizes, roll in the sugar and flatten into cookie sheet. Bake for 12 minutes at 350 degrees.

Doughnuts

- 2 eggs beaten
- 1 1/4 cups of sugar
- 3 cups of flour
- 1 1/2 teaspoons of salt

- 3 teaspoons of cream of tarter
- 1 1/2 teaspoons of soda
- 1 teaspoon of nutmeg
- 1 cup of milk

Slowly add flour to mixture to make soft dough. Roll out doughnuts (do not allow dough to stand for long). Fry in deep fat.

Creature Pie

- graham cracker crust
- 1 tablespoon gelatine
- 4 tablespoons cold water
- 2 tablespoons of rum
- 4 egg yolks

- 4 egg whites
- 1/3 cup sugar
- 1/2 cup boiling water
- 1/2 teaspoon salt
- 1/2 teaspoon nutmeg

Soak the gelatine in the rum and cold water. Beat eggs until fluffy, with sugar and salt mixed in. Add boiling water and cook to a custard, then pour hot custard over gelatine and rum. Stir to dissolve gelatine. Add nutmeg, and chill. Beat egg whites until stiff, adding sugar. Add custard to whites, pour into crust and chill.

Bibliography

Board of Park Commissioners. *A Reference Guide to Salem, 1630,* The City of Salem, Massachusetts, 1959.

Botkin, B.A. *A Treasury of New England Folklore,* American Legacy Press, New York, 1965.

Chambers, Thomas K. *Lessons in Cookery,* D. Appleton & Co., New York, 1879.

Club, The. *Sketches About Salem People,* Newcomb & Gauss Company, Salem, Massachusetts, 1930.

Dow, George Francis. *Every Day Life in the Massachusetts Bay Colony,* Dover Publications, Inc., New York, 1988.

Drake, Samuel Adams. *Nooks and Corners of the New England Coast,* Harper and Bros. Publishers, New York, 1875.

Hendrickson, Robert. *The Great American Tomato Book,* Doubleday & Co., Garden City, New York, 1977.

Hill, Paul and Mavis. *The Edible Sea,* A.S. Barnes & Co., Cranbury, New Jersey, 1975.

Knight, Sarah Kemble. *Journal,* Boston, Massachusetts, 1704.

Larcum, Lucy. *A New England Girlhood,* Houghton-Mifflin Co., Boston, 1890.

Larkin, Jack. *The Reshaping of Everyday Life in the United States, 1790-1840,* Harper & Row, New York, 1988.

Lawrence, Robert Means. *New England Colonial Life,* The Cosmos Press, Inc., Cambridge, Massachusetts, 1927.

Morison, Samuel Eliot. *Builders of the Bay Colony,* Houghton-Mifflin Co., Boston, 1930.

Murphy, Edward F. *Yankee Priest,* The Country Life Press, Garden City, New York, 1952

Phillips, James Duncan. *Pepper and Pirates,* The Riverside Press, Cambridge, Massachusetts, 1949.

Phillips, James Duncan. *Salem in the Eighteenth Century,* The Riverside Press, Cambridge, Massachusetts, 1969.

Putnam, George Granville. *Salem Vessels and Their Voyages, Volumes I-IV,* The Essex Institute, Salem, Massachusetts, 1924.

Salem Garden Club, The. *Old Salem Gardens,* Salem, Massachusetts, 1946.

Sharkey, Olive. *Old Days, Old Ways,* Syracuse University Press, Syracuse, New York, 1987.

Simpson, George. *A Book About A Thousand Things,* Harper & Bros. Publishers, New York, 1946.

Society for the Preservation of New England Antiquities. *Old-Time New England,* Boston, Massachusetts, 1957.

Trustees of Boston University. *Foodways in the Northeast*, Boston University, Boston, 1984.

Ulrich, Laurel Thatcher. *A Midwife's Tale,* Alfred A. Knopf, New York, 1990.

We Were New England, Stackpole Sons, 1937.

Willison, George F. *Saints and Strangers,* Ballantine Books, New York, 1945.